BLANDING PUBLIC LIBRARY

GOFF MEMORIAL PARISH HOUSE
REHOBOTH, MASS.

HOURS
Monday 2-4:30 P.M.
Tuesday 6-9 P.M.
Wednesday 2-4:30 P.M.
Thursday 6-9 P.M.
Saturday 1-5 P.M.

1. This book may be kept fourteen days.
2. Books overdue incur a fine of two cents a day.
3. Books lost or damaged must be paid for.

YOUNG BOOKER

Booker T. Washington's Early Days

Selected List of Other Books by Arna Bontemps

STORY OF THE NEGRO

WE HAVE TOMORROW

CHARIOT IN THE SKY

GOLDEN SLIPPERS *(Anthology)*

BLACK THUNDER

GOD SENDS SUNDAY

100 YEARS OF NEGRO FREEDOM

AMERICAN NEGRO POETRY *(Anthology)*

FAMOUS NEGRO ATHLETES

HOLD FAST TO DREAMS *(Anthology)*

GREAT SLAVE NARRATIVES *(Anthology)*

FREE AT LAST: *The Life of Frederick Douglass*

HARLEM RENAISSANCE REMEMBERED *(Editor)*

With Jack Conroy

THE FAST SOONER HOUND

THEY SEEK A CITY

Edited by Langston Hughes and Arna Bontemps

THE BOOK OF NEGRO FOLKLORE

THE POETRY OF THE NEGRO (1746–1970)

YOUNG BOOKER

Booker T. Washington's Early Days

BY

ARNA BONTEMPS

ILLUSTRATED WITH PHOTOGRAPHS

DODD, MEAD & COMPANY

NEW YORK

ISBN: 0–396–06514–7

Library of Congress Catalog Card Number: 72–3724
Printed in the United States of America
by The Cornwall Press, Inc., Cornwall, N.Y.

To Owen A. Troy, Jr.

CONTENTS

ILLUSTRATIONS

* With the exception of these two photographs, all pictures are courtesy of the Hollis Burke Frissell Library, Tuskegee Institute.

YOUNG BOOKER

Booker T. Washington's Early Days

I

JOURNEY

NOTHING about the boy's appearance was remarkable, and few strangers who saw him in the big road headed toward Richmond that autumn day bothered to take a second glance. A stray, buff-colored sixteen year old, poorly dressed and carrying his belongings in a cheap satchel, walking when he had to, begging rides when he could, was no novelty in the South of 1872. The War had upset everything, and seven years after it ended there were still many homeless children of slaves on the Virginia roads. Most of them, not unlike some of the impoverished, dislocated children of their former masters, had only vague notions as to where they were going or what they wanted to do. But going places helped. Movement healed their loneliness, helped to soothe the lost feeling. Misery had a lot of company on the big roads in those days, and in that throng the boy called Booker passed unnoticed. Even those folk who let him toss his satchel into their empty wagons and hop on the back to ride a short piece failed to detect the subtle difference between this wanderer and the rest. Booker knew where he was going and what he wanted, and the look in his eyes, the set of his chin, and the way he held his mouth showed that he was deadly serious.

He had not started his journey by foot. There had been a train out of Malden, and he had ridden as far as it went. Stagecoaches had brought him a right smart distance over the mountains of West Virginia and might have taken him all the way into Richmond had not his money run out. Just before the last of it was spent, however, his eyes had been strangely opened in a way that they could never be closed again.

The stage on which he rode had come to a stop in front of a rough, unpainted house among the hills. Twilight fell as the tired travelers stretched the kinks out of their legs and started toward the door. Booker heard someone call the place a hotel, but he did not know what the word meant till he entered and saw the other passengers standing before a man at a desk and arranging for rooms and meals. As one after another was shown to his quarters and told what the charges would be, the uneasy boy began wondering what he would say when his turn came. He was sure the few coins remaining in his pocket could not cover it, and the question in his mind was how to offer the landlord services instead. Perhaps he could chop wood or wash dishes. Outside the night air was already cool, and the excitement of Booker's adventure no longer obscured the fact that the body needed food. He was powerfully hungry. When everyone else had been assigned and the man was alone at the desk, the boy picked up his bag and stepped forward, his speech ready.

But he did not get a chance to open his mouth. The landlord put down his pen and spat the brutal words at the colored boy. Booker was more puzzled than wounded, more troubled about the prospect of a chilly night outdoors than by the offense to his pride, but nine years of slavery and seven years of new freedom in Virginia and West Virginia had not prepared him for segregation. He had never seen it or heard about it. That the proprietor should reject him without even asking whether or not he had enough money to pay for lodging seemed somehow unreal to Booker as he went outdoors to stroll the mountain paths and ponder in the darkness.

Intrigued as he had been by this novel experience, he had nevertheless found it impossible to keep his mind on it. Personal irritations or discomforts no longer counted. Wherever else his thoughts dwelt momentarily, they were promptly drawn again as by a magnet to his destination. Nothing mattered so long as he got there whole.

But the city of Richmond was nowhere in sight when he boarded the stage again the next morning. When the last of his money was gone and he commenced walking, the city was still a long way off. Hampton, he understood, was beyond that. Far beyond. And so he had continued, as now, tramping out the miles, resting by the roadside when weary, sleeping on the ground at night, trying to reach the big city before he became too famished to walk.

He was fit to drop in his tracks when he finally arrived. Night had fallen, and an air of mystery seemed to hang over the sprawling community. Booker had never before seen a big city. His need of rest and food, however, was anything but mysterious. He began following his nose up and down the streets, tantalized by cooking odors and glimpses of food stands where "fried chicken and half-moon apples pies were piled high and made to present a most tempting appearance." He knew nothing about urban life, but he understood that these were not for a boy without money, and it was not till he had been refused several times that he gave up the hope of finding someone hospitable enough to take him in for the night or trusting enough to accept his pledge to work and pay later. Perhaps his appearance was partly to blame.

Clothes which had been only moderately shabby at home had deteriorated steadily on the road. Booker looked like a tramp. Not knowing what else to do after the city went to sleep, he kept trudging. When he could no longer drag one foot after the other, he noticed that the board sidewalk on which he stood was somewhat elevated. Either the ground had been washed out beneath it or the walk had been constructed so as to bridge a ditch. What impressed Booker was simply dark space—space in which to crawl out of sight. He paused to make sure he was not being watched, stepped down from the walk, shoved his satchel under, and wormed in after it on his belly.

In his sleep Booker heard feet walking over his head. When he opened his eyes to daylight, he remembered where he was and understood the tramping. He felt better after the rest, but his stomach was still in a knot. Peeping from under the boards, he made sure no one was looking and then rolled out, leaving the satchel of clothes behind. Soon the morning haze cleared, and he began to explore cautiously.

The river was nearby with a large ship docked at the landing. Up and down its gangplank went dark figures in the mist. They seemed to be unloading something heavy. Was it pig iron? Booker approached the vessel and began looking for the head man. A kindly white captain listened to his story and then nodded.

Though people were generally inclined to listen when he spoke and to believe what he said, Booker was particularly grateful to this one. In another minute he was on the gangplank with the other rousters, stepping on the heels of the one in front of him. When he thought he had done enough to warrant it, he approached the captain and asked if he might collect a little money with which to buy breakfast. The captain agreed, and Booker took time out to fill his stomach.

Never within memory had food tasted so good, but there was no time to waste. Booker finished his meal and hurried back to the ship. At the close of the day the captain suggested that if the boy wished to continue working at a small daily wage, he might do so. Even when he multiplied the cost of the meal he had just eaten by three and figured that the profit would be small, Booker still liked the idea. By saving the remainder each day he would eventually be able to continue his journey, and that was what counted. Naturally he would have to continue to sleep under the wooden sidewalk.

Even so, nights passed quickly. And the days—well, they passed too, and when he had accumulated enough money, Booker paid his respects to the old captain and caught a train.

2.

The village of Hampton showed its age. Many of the larger houses, surrounded by clusters of whitewashed cabins, seemed ready to topple. The quaint, two-hundred-year-old church of St. John was a ruin, its graveyard deserted. An ancient courthouse and other public buildings were still erect, however, and the meadow on which they stood reached to the west bank of a widening stream. Beyond—and not too far beyond—was the blue bay in which, ten years earlier, the made-over Confederate ironclad *Merrimac* had knocked out the Union's *Cumberland*, and then on the following day, as crowds of dark folk along the shore watched and prayed for her defeat, taken her own lumps before running away from the black-turreted avenger, the *Monitor*.

Fortress Monroe and Old Point Comfort were in the same direction, both looking out on Hampton Roads, with its swarms of oyster boats and singing Negro boatmen. It was toward them that Booker walked from the village on the morning of his arrival. Nothing he saw or heard along the way detained him. History, recent or remote, was all alike to him. His interest was in the present, and the chilling fact of the moment was the fifty cents which jingled in his pockets. It was all that remained of his earnings on the waterfront.

He had not gone far when the three-story, red brick building of the Hampton Normal and Agricultural Institute loomed ahead. Standing near the water's edge, surrounded by a half dozen wooden cottages, the Stars and Stripes waving handsomely from a tall flagpole, it seemed to the grimey, exhausted Booker a spectacle of sheer majesty. But how did you enter a school like this? Who did you see? What did you say?

Of one thing he was sure. A new phase of his life had begun. There was nothing in the past—the past he didn't even want to think about—to which he could return, now that he had reached Hampton Institute. The anxiety of the journey, the weeks of weariness and hunger on the road had been amply rewarded by the first glimpse, but he could not stand there and feast his eyes. He had to do something.

Suddenly he felt an urgent need to achieve, to win out over difficulties, to make something of his life, to be worthy of Hampton, to possess the dream. He moved uneasily on the grounds till he met someone who could direct him to the "head teacher." When he was finally shown into her presence, he found that he was not the only new student seeking admission. Miss Mary F. Mackie, a typical New England schoolmarm, was besieged by hopeful applicants trying in ridiculous ways to impress her with their worthiness.

Most of them were actually adults. Freedom made them feel young and hopeful again. Some thought they should behave like children, but Booker saw that Miss Mackie's shrewd yankee eyes were not deluded. She calmly rejected many more than she accepted. When his turn came, he was definitely worried.

Miss Mackie's first reaction was not good. Booker read the expression on her face and decided that his appearance was against him. He had slept too many nights on the ground in the clothes he was wearing. If the Yankee lady took him for a bum, he couldn't rightly blame her. But neither could he let the matter rest there, not now—not after the journey he had made. Miss Mackie was about to say no when suddenly she hesitated. Booker might wait, she indicated. She wasn't sure. She needed more time to make up her mind.

As he waited he saw others accepted, and Booker watched for a chance to show what he was worth. Minutes passed. They ran into hours, and Booker squirmed as he saw students admitted whom he knew instinctively were not superior to himself. Finally, the New England prejudice against dirt and uncleanness still dominant in her thought, Miss Mackie called him to her desk again.

"The adjoining recitation-room needs sweeping," she said, pointing. "Take the broom and sweep it."

The command excited Booker. *Broom. Sweep.* He had cleaned house for a Yankee woman before, back in Malden, West Virginia. He knew what they demanded. If this was to be his test, if his chance to enter Hampton as a student depended on it, he would show the "head teacher" some sweeping and cleaning that would make her head spin. With a kind of fury he went into the room and closed the door.

While he resented her inclination to judge him by his ragged and dirty clothes, he held no bitterness toward Miss Mackie. If keeping clean was that important to some people —well, he knew what to do. Dust began to fly. Furniture was moved. The closet doors were opened, everything inside brought out. Once, twice, three times Booker swept the room. Then, convinced that there was nothing else a broom could find, he replaced the desk, chairs, and table and began dusting.

He dusted high and low, the woodwork on the walls, the chairs and tables, every possible surface on which dirt particles could settle. When he finished, he started all over again. He dusted the room four times, in fact, before he was ready to face Miss Mackie again and report the job done.

The stern woman did not speak. Instead she rose from her desk and led Booker back to the classroom. She headed straight for the closet, opened the door, examined the shelves and the floor. Then she took out her small white handkerchief, reached high against the wall and rubbed against the woodwork. When she found no dust there, she rubbed it over the table and the benches. Still austere and unsmiling she turned to the speechless boy.

"I guess you will do to enter this institution."

3.

Booker was so elated he could have lept into the air. The janitor work to which he was assigned would pay for most of his board and keep at Hampton. The balance—the cost of clothes, the seventy dollars a year required for tuition— well, one step at a time. Booker put down his fifty cents on account and went to work proudly.

Between attending classes, which did not seem to make much impression on him at first, cleaning a long string of rooms, building fires at four o'clock in the morning and preparing lessons, Booker soon found himself head-over-heels in his new occupation. Up late and early, he scarcely had time to sleep. While he had never hoped for a bed of roses, the Hampton ordeal for a boy without money turned out to be more rugged than even Booker had expected. He groaned but he did not flinch, and presently he found himself looking into the benign face of a hero whose nobility of character was so apparent it made all tasks seem light.

General Samuel Chapman Armstrong, a thirty-three-year-old soldier-teacher, seemed to the boy from Malden a Christ-like figure. The white men Booker had known in slavery and later around the mines of West Virginia had not prepared him for acquaintance with a man of Armstrong's qualities. In the founder of Hampton Institute an understanding of human frailty and a sympathy with human need were not inconsistent with zeal for orderliness and discipline. Booker felt like a small, wandering star that had just floated into the orbit of a new sun. His first impulse was a desire to do "something real hard for the General."

Only later did he learn what had gone into the making of the character that had so suddenly altered his outlook, but Booker's loyalty was committed on the spot and for life. When he learned more, the commitment was merely reaffirmed with specific reference to Armstrong's educational theories and his general attitude toward life and the society in which he lived. In short, Booker became a disciple and went about his duties at Hampton asking himself over and over again, "What would the General say to this?" or "How would the General like that?" and actually resenting time spent with books that might have been spent in Armstrong's presence. In young Booker's eyesight Samuel Chapman Armstrong glittered when he walked.

The soldierly man with the soft eyes had been born of missionary parents in Hawaii. While his father held a theological degree from Washington College of Lexington, Virginia, young Armstrong had been sent to Williams, from which he was graduated in the summer of 1862. He had entered the Union Army as a captain of a New York regiment but had later been transferred to the Eighth Regiment of U.S. Colored Troops and commissioned colonel. Mustered out as brigadier general by brevet at the close of the War, he had been appointed chief official of the Freedman's Bureau at Hampton, Virginia. His experience with Negro soldiers and emancipated slaves, coupled with the missionary influences of his childhood home among the Island folk of Hawaii, was the foundation of the educational enterprise he had begun at Hampton two years after Appomattox.

Even before the War ended, the American Missionary Association had undertaken educational work in behalf of freedmen. That slave children, if not indeed their elders, would have to be taught to live on their own responsibility seemed to go without saying. As early as 1863 a school for fugitives was conducted at Fortress Monroe behind Union lines. Later the Society of Friends in the North had sent several teachers to the vicinity of Hampton and conducted an orphanage in a deserted house, till they were overwhelmed by sixteen hundred lost children seeking care. In January of 1867 the

American Missionary Magazine published an article by General Armstrong offering a new approach to the problem. It turned out to be the blueprint for Hampton Normal and Agricultural Institute.

Armstrong's plan of vocational education for the freedmen in the United States and for the training of teachers to fan out among the communities of the South was an adaptation of an idea developed by missionaries in Hawaii. Stress was placed on inculcating habits useful for citizenship. The first aim was to teach self-respect, industry, and discipline. Since time was an important factor, a short curriculum was indicated. The founders of Hampton projected a three-year course in which the study of books was given such place as its secondary importance allowed.

Booker absorbed the philosophy of the program as readily and as eagerly as he adopted the ritual of a daily bath, clean shirts and socks (washed nightly for wearing the next day), the enchantment of a toothbrush, sleeping between sheets, eating on a tablecloth at regular hours, and using a napkin—all of which were startlingly new to him. Almost instantly he detected a relationship between cleanliness of the body and self-respect, between physical and mental health, and he liked what he discerned. Splashing gleefully in his tub, he knew he had plopped into a way of life suited to his nature.

He also knew instinctively that certain hard realities in connection with his situation would have to be met and dealt with soon. Board at Hampton, including room and the other living costs, was ten dollars a month. He had been told at the beginning that his job as a janitor would pay for only a part of this expense, and he did not have to be told that the fifty cents he had put down with his registration would not take care of the balance. Nor could he long close his eyes to the fact that the seventy dollars for his yearly tuition would have to be paid somehow if he were to remain in school at Hampton.

What he did not know as he racked his brain, writing without hope to the brother he had left in Malden, was that General Armstrong was now watching him with a gleam of discovery. The boy the General saw, scrubbed and improved since his arrival on the grounds, was pleasing in appearance but still not one to draw immediate attention to himself. He was of medium size, nervously alert but not fidgety, light brown in color, with reddish brown hair. His cheek bones were high and prominent, his nose wide, his mouth large and full-lipped, his chin firm—a face the spit'n image of which was to reappear dramatically in Detroit sixty years later when Americans first became aware of young Joe Louis. Only Booker's eyes were different. If it was not ancient wisdom that General Armstrong saw reflected in them, it was something equally remarkable.

Nothing that he observed about the boy in the next few weeks or months caused the General to question that early impression, and when the showdown eventually came, he quietly informed the youth that a vague Mr. S. Griffitts Morgan of New Bedford, Massachusetts, had kindly consented to pay his tuition. Booker T. Washington would remain at Hampton.

4.

Again it seemed for a time that all obstacles were cleared from his way, but the effect of daily washing on his single shirt, the drying before the fire of his one pair of socks, soon made him aware of other problems. The clothes in which he went to class, did his janitor work, and dressed up, as occasion required, were deteriorating rapidly; and the fact that John, Booker's brother back in Malden, had begun to pinch off small sums from his meager earnings as a laborer and to send them at long intervals to apply on Booker's board deficit only served to highlight Booker's need of clothes.

But General Armstrong and the other teachers at Hampton, now entering upon the fifth year of their program to teach self-reliance and resourcefulness to former slaves, knew to what extent they could expect the young people to help themselves. While they left Booker and others like him to wrestle with their problems, they did not themselves cease working in the students' behalf. Again it was by their efforts rather than his own that Booker was rescued. This time a barrel of second-hand clothing from the North, the gift of charitable church folk, was the lifesaver.

Booker blinked with amazement as he received an allotment. Now he could go to his room, sew on buttons, polish his ill-fitting shoes, do a little washing and pressing, and be ready for the daily inspection to which General Armstrong subjected all Hampton students. Now—now he could feel at ease with the six other boys whose room he shared. The others had been in school longer than he and knew better what to do and what to expect. Now he could begin to learn a few things from them. The puzzling matter of the two sheets on the bed, for example. Did you sleep under them or on top of them? With misgivings Booker had tried both ways, and it was a pleasant discovery to learn that these more experienced boys slept between the sheets. That was for him too—from now on. And if ever he got the chance, he would tell the whole nation that it was a fine idea. More folk should know about it.

Looking at his fellow students, Booker began to make other observations. Most of them were considerably older than himself. A student of forty was not uncommon at Hampton then. Too old to learn readily from books, most of them made up for this deficiency by sheer zeal. They had seen enough of life to know the practical value of education, and the fact that a number of them had dependent families, worn-out parents at home, wives with young children, made them just that much more determined to succeed. They were out to make up time and they gave Hampton's student body of from four to five hundred a tremendous incentive. To Booker the air seemed electric.

Such racing and hurrying, such eagerness to please teachers, such exaggerated efforts to win acceptance and then perhaps make oneself necessary, if not indispensable, he had never seen nor even imagined, but he fell in with the general trend. He did not mean to be left behind. That winter, for example, when the dormitory space became overcrowded as a result of more and more students imploring admission, General Armstrong had tents pitched in front of the men's building and asked for volunteers to help him solve the space problem by moving into them. Nearly every male student of the Institute stepped forward, but none more alertly than Booker, and he was among those on whom the painful honor fell.

Never in his experience had a winter been so cruel. Winds lifted the tent in which he slept completely off the ground, roaring through the opening. But when the General walked among the cots at daybreak, greeting the stiffened, corpselike volunteers with words of cheer, praising their valor, they belittled their discomfort and lept into their pants like true soldiers. Down in his heart a strange little fire warmed

Booker. The idea of doing something to please his hero, something painful and hard, kept him from freezing to death.

Meanwhile more barrels of second-hand clothes arrived from the North. Booker got a chance to dip into several of these, with the result that raiment, cut and fit aside, ceased to be the most urgent of his needs. Indeed, as spring came and school closing loomed ahead, he had an extra coat of rather good quality which he treasured as money in the bank. And when the other students began talking of going home or doing this or that during the summer, plans and projects completely beyond the reach of the penniless Booker, a thought occurred to him. If he could sell his extra coat, perhaps he could realize enough from it to pay his fare back to Malden. He too could then get busy with summer plans, could talk of going home and greeting his loved ones, could hold up his head and hide from his fellow students the fact that he was at his wit's end with no real notion of what to do with himself during the vacation period.

When other students began actually to leave the campus, Booker was overcome by feelings of loneliness and loss. Only the coat gave him hope. He watched for his chance to go into the town of Hampton and circulate among men of the kind he thought might be interested in acquiring such a garment. Resistance to his offer was stronger then he had anticipated, but eventually he found one Negro he could entice with a verbal description of the coat, and with considerable effort Booker bound him to a promise to come out to the Institute and have a look at it.

The man knocked at his door in the dormitory the next morning, and Booker proudly took the coat from its hook. The man's eyes brightened. How much?

Booker considered. How about three dollars, he ventured.

"I tell you what I'll do," the man from town proposed. "I'll take the coat, and I'll pay you five cents, cash down, and pay you the rest of the money just as soon as I can get it."

Booker closed the door. His hopes for a visit home died with the footsteps down the hall. When his spirit revived somewhat, he went into the town again and began looking for work. Not only did he need money to keep him alive during the summer, but what troubled him even more was a sixteen-dollar indebtedness to Hampton above what he had been able to pay by work and by the small contributions from his brother John. Until he could find a way of paying this, he resolved, he would not present himself again for admission to the school. He was convinced that his honor was at stake.

Several hot, discouraging days of job hunting ended when a restaurant at Fortress Monroe offered him work. The wages were almost nothing, however, and Booker found that after his board had been deducted, the balance was not enough to save. On the other hand, his tasks were light, and between meals and at night there was time to think and read. Booker did a great deal of each that summer and felt a certain exhilaration as a result, but as August drew to an end, he could not help remembering that the sixteen dollars against him remained on Hampton's books, and his heart sank.

Then one day a miracle happened. While he was clearing the dirty dishes from a table, his eyes fell upon a crisp, new, ten-dollar bill on the floor. He nearly fainted with joy. On second thought he decided to tell the proprietor about it. Perhaps that individual would be made happy too, considering the skimpy wage he had paid.

But while the man laughed, Booker detected a strange light in his eye. A moment later he discovered the cause. The proprietor was grateful, sincerely grateful, but he would have

Booker remember who owned this restaurant. A piece of money found in it belonged rightly to the owner. He would thank the helper to hand it over.

5.

The jolt did not discourage him, for Booker was not susceptible to discouragement. Something within him automatically rejected the notion of failure. If he had learned any one thing in the early years of his life, it was that strategy was the key to success. One moved toward his goals as he found the proper approach or adopted the right formula. He stood still or lost ground when he was going at it wrong. In which case the only thing to do was to try something else. There was a way to get ahead in life. Of that Booker was certain.

And there was bound to be a way for him to continue at Hampton despite the sixteen-dollar charge against his first year's expenses. Throughout the summer he had insisted to himself that he would not return without money to put down before the cold, demanding eyes of General J. F. B. Marshall, the Institute's treasurer. But the incident of the ten-dollar bill shook him enough to cause him to reconsider that resolve. He now decided to return to Hampton and tell the treasurer what had happened.

To Booker's surprise, General Marshall told him that the debt would not prevent him from beginning his second year. He could have his janitor job back, and the treasurer would trust him to repay the sixteen dollars when he could. It was all settled so simply and quickly that it seemed to change Booker's whole outlook on his work at Hampton.

His second year began immediately to be marked by a kind

of awakening. Booker began to notice the missionary zeal of the Hampton teachers, their unselfish commitment to a work that promised very little in return. He concluded that they must have found rewards that did not meet the eye, some sort of satisfactions obtained only through doing things for other people, and he concluded that that was something he too would like to try.

He began to find time to discover the Hampton farm. He had not previously noticed the oxen, the horses, the chickens and ducks raised there. Now he observed a marked difference between the breeds at Hampton and those he had seen in barnyards near his boyhood home. Never again would he admire droopy, tail-dragging fowl, scrawny, undersized live-stock. The fine breeds were for him.

In that second year he came under the influence of still another inspiring teacher. Miss Natalie Lord was from Portland, Maine. In her class he began to enjoy reading the Bible. As he had heard the scriptures read before, by the preacher in the Baptist Church in Malden and by Sunday-school teachers, Booker had never found them very interesting. Miss Lord opened the book to passages he never dreamed it contained. He liked the stories and parables, but he also enjoyed the wise sayings and felt a spiritual boost in the poety.

Though he did not absorb the Bible to the point of quoting it offhand or borrowing from its imagery, Booker formed the habit of reading in the book daily, and more and more often thereafter he found himself thinking and expressing himself in parables and proverbs of his own making.

Miss Lord noticed Booker's readiness to stand up before the other students of the class, his natural ease of self-expression on these occasions. She thought she detected something worth encouraging. Would Booker like a little help outside of class in the principles of public speaking? While he could think of nothing that appealed to him less than elocution or speaking for its own sake, Booker readily accepted. He assumed that Miss Lord had in mind instruction that would improve his power to influence people through platform discourse, to tell the world some of the things that were beginning to crowd his mind.

He was not disappointed. The lessons were practical and helpful, and they led him to participate more actively in the Saturday night sessions of Hampton's several debating societies. Indeed, he became so excited about this extracurricular activity that he got an idea for still another society. When the men students left the dining room after supper, there was a hiatus of about twenty minutes in the schedule which permitted them to relax in any way they wished till the beginning of the evening study period. Generally this time was filled with idle talk or wasted in other ways, Booker felt. His idea was to assemble about twenty fellow students and turn the interlude into a daily session for practicing debate and public address. Soon this period became the brightest spot in Booker's day, and his second year at Hampton slipped by with astonishing swiftness.

Apparently his account with the school was in order this time, for small gifts of money received from his mother in Malden and from his brother John, along with one from one of his teachers at Hampton, were set aside by Booker for train and coach fare home at the close of school. He had not seen his hometown or his relatives in nearly two years, and memories of them had grown increasingly poignant. The dismal summer in the restaurant at Fortress Monroe was also vivid in his thoughts. He certainly did not want to spend another vacation in the same fashion.

Malden was home. His mother was there, his warmhearted, selfless mother; and the word Booker had from John was that she had not been well since he left. Remembering her at Hampton, Booker stopped in his tracks and surrendered himself to an emotion he would not have dared indulge had he lacked the means to get home or had the school term not been near a close. He could think about her now, because soon he would be standing on the doorstep, and she would have her face on his shoulder. The others would stand around, waiting to shake his hand or kiss his cheek. His stepfather, his young sister Amanda, John—he had been too long away from all of them.

His dream now was to be a man of some account so that he could give his mother things for her comfort and find ways to make her happy. When he was a child, he recalled, she had sighed deeply when she expressed the hope that God would let her live to see her children educated and started in life. In his dream Booker saw himself working so hard and achieving so well his mother would have to smile. Shadows would leave her breast and fly away like ugly birds disappearing in the black of night.

6.

Booker had scarcely alighted from the train when he became aware of a tenseness in the air. The salt furnaces of Malden were not running. The men were out on strike. Labor troubles between the workers and the operators could not detain

Booker today, however. Suitcase in hand, he swiftly brushed past the idle men on the streets.

A few moments later a gaunt, black woman clasped him in her arms in the doorway of the shack he called home. He scarcely noticed how wasted and changed she was, but his mother's tearful rejoicing seemed to him "almost pathetic." Though he had been homesick himself, he was not prepared for such overwhelming emotion. It was as if the frail woman had lived only for his return. He could have cried as she clung to him, and the family and neighbors gathered in the front room and around the doorstep.

Neat and clean and togged out in clothes that came to Hampton in barrels, Booker gave the home folks a quick demonstration of the improvements two years can make in a boy under the right conditions. They looked him over critically, and when he spoke to them familiarly in the grave but understanding tone they remembered, showing that the personality they loved was still intact, they suddenly gave him their approval. Education was good. He had passed their test.

For the next few days he was at their mercy. His family, the neighbors—all wanted to hear his story. They let him alone while he sat at the table, eating the good food his mother cooked, but as soon as his plate was empty they insisted on hearing his experiences at Hampton, and he told them about the two sheets on each bed, the daily baths, the white teachers from fine families up North who did not mind working with their hands between classes, the perfect man, General Armstrong. He told them about his journey, the troubles he had getting to Hampton, about the little things he had to learn in school and about the way he had spent his last summer. When he finished, John and Amanda and their stepfather were so excited they ran around telling their cousins and friends what marvelous stories Booker had brought home with him.

Thereafter he had to go the rounds, eating a meal with each family and repeating his stories at each table. When it seemed that all who wanted to hear him could not be reached in this way, arrangements were made for him to tell his experiences in the Baptist Sunday school in which he had grown up, and that went over just as well as the private accounts. Indeed, the old folks who listened to his talk were soon quite beside themselves with pride and joy. Without any special effort to impress, Booker had fairly hypnotized them. He was their boy all right, this deadpan, quietly humorous son of mining folk. He could never be anything else but their boy. No matter where he went or what he did or what happened to him, he was theirs.

For the next few days it was Booker, Booker, Booker, wherever he turned. Then he decided this sort of thing had gone on long enough. He put on his working clothes and went out to find a job. Friendly words, fatted calf, and welcome-home talk were all well and good in their place—in fact, they were wonderful—but they would not of themselves put money in his pocket. They could not help him return to Hampton. It was now time to hit the ball—and hit it hard. Booker headed for the coal mines.

To his surprise, the mine was not operating. The strike of the men employed in the salt furnaces had been the first thing he noticed when he got off the train, but then the delirious ritual of homecoming had begun, and while that lasted there had been no occasion to ask what effect the strike in the salt furnaces was having on the operations in the coal mine. Perhaps the idleness of the miners he knew had seemed like part of a general holiday in his honor. In any case, he knew better now. He could expect no work in the coal mine that summer.

Booker began looking for something else. He would have to earn at least enough money to pay his way back to Hampton, and he had set his heart on putting aside some for the extra needs of school life, denial of which could sometimes be so painful, but the first few days of his search convinced him that success was by no means a foregone conclusion. Long periods of walking the streets followed, with Booker growing more and more anxious about the final year of his schooling and more and more bitter about the strike that had put such a serious crimp in his summer plans. Disappointed and tired, he began forming an attitude toward strikes and strikers. The villian? The professional labor agitator, Booker decided.

Within a few weeks all the happiness of his return to Malden went sour. No place in the whole community was there a job at which he could work for pay that summer, and a third of the vacation had slipped away while he pounded the streets. Then one day, as the wasted first month came to a close, he decided to explore the countryside a few miles beyond the surrounding hills. He rose early, and he went as far as he thought he could safely venture in one day and still return home that night. But when he found no work immediately, he continued to search. When darkness fell, he was so tired and so far from Malden, he wandered into a deserted, bat-haunted house and fell on the floor.

Into his sleep heavy footsteps blundered suddenly. Was it a dream that awakened him? Another wayfarer? A returning owner of the abandoned property? An officer of the law? A stuttering, high-pitched voice, distressed and out of breath, reassured the sleeper. What was his brother John doing here?

Why had he come so far? How had he found Booker at this ungodly hour, in this decaying place? John dropped to his knees and broke into tears.

Their mother was dead. John had come across the hills at three o'clock in the morning to find his younger brother and give him this heartbreaking news. Booker stretched out on the floor again. For a long time he did not answer.

II

SONG OF THE SON

SUDDENLY he could smell the windowless cabin in which he had slept in her arms as an infant. Where was it? When?

Three small creatures had squirmed against her body like the troubled litter of a farm beast. She knew why they whimpered, the three-year-old Booker, his younger sister, and older brother, and she had a way of shaking them from her when she could endure their fretting no longer. Leaving them among their rags on the dirt floor, she would crawl to the door of the cabin and disappear in the night. How long she would be gone at such times, the drowsy Booker could not imagine, but he still remembered vividly how he would sometimes awaken from wretched, gnawing sleep to a feast of steaming chicken or fried eggs. He could not forget the fine glow of warm coals over which she did her cooking.

Now he could understand why this had happened only at night. *Stealing* was an ugly word, as he had learned even before going to Hampton, but the plantation on which Booker was born, near Hales Ford in Franklin County, Virginia, was no place for moralizing. The female's instinct to feed her young did not stand on ceremony. Even if it had, the

25

slave mind was capable cf rationalizing. Jane, as she was called, belonged to old master. Booker, Amanda, and John belonged to master too, and so did the chickens, the eggs, the corn, and everything else on the plantation. If one of master's slaves ate one of master's chickens, who had been robbed? What had old master lost? In fact, what could be more profitable to him than for a mother slave to keep her children alive?

After freedom, Booker recalled, Jane had shown that she hated lying and thieving as much as anybody. Nor had she winked her eye, since emancipation, at that which from the pulpit of the little Baptist Church was called adultery. The fact that she was velvety black and that he and John were tea-colored was too noticeable to be ignored. His reddish-brown hair and gray eyes required an explanation. Yet nothing Booker could remember or surmise allowed him to think of his mother as anything but a saint.

He had learned very young that she was married to a slave husband from another plantation, who was not Booker's father. Jane's husband was allowed to visit her no oftener than once a year, but their devotion to each other had never been questioned. Things happened to slaves and among slaves that could not be clearly judged apart from slavery. His own birth, apparently, was such a happening. But who was his father?

Jane had told him only that "he was a white man." Now she was dead with her secret, and only God could foretell the irony to come. Twenty years after her death, when her light brown son had become the best-known, by many called the greatest, American born south of the Mason-Dixon line since the Civil War, more than one white family thereabouts planted the suspicion that a naughty uncle or brother of theirs had jumped that particular fence on the evening in question. But Booker thought of nothing so improbable the night of her passing. His mind was too crowded with realities.

Morning light broke through the cracks of the cabin, he recalled, and the 4′ x 16′ interior reappeared dimly. The fireplace at which Jane, the big-house cook, prepared food for the master's family as well as for her own, the deep hole in the dirt floor in which sweet potatoes for the master's table were kept during the winter, the topsy-turvy heap of rags on which Jane slept with her young—he could see them all again.

After a time the question of clothing arose. Even slaves did not continue to run around a plantation buck naked when they were past five or six years old. Booker knew he would never, never forget his first garment. It was called a "tow" shirt, and the thing about it that made it memorable was that it was made of refuse flax. The fiber was stiff and coarse. Until it had been worn six weeks or more, it pricked the flesh with a thousand little pinpoints. No, Booker would never forget the day he put his first one on.

It had been in wartime, he knew. The families of planters as well as the troops of the Confederacy had suffered a clothing shortage. Naturally their worst was the slave's best. Being accustomed to hardships, however, the folk in the quarters probably felt it no more acutely than did those in the great house, but the sheer problem of hiding the private parts of their bodies kept them at their wit's end. That Booker should have reached the age of decency, so to speak, at such a time was a double misfortune.

He cried so loud and persistently in his misery, in fact, that he awakened the sympathy of his brother John. Day after day the older boy looked on with feeling as his little brother wriggled out of the "instrument of torture" to reveal a lemon-colored body reddened by the scratching of the flax. Finally, when he could stand it no longer, John offered to swap shirts with Booker and to wear the new one till it was broken in. Booker was not ungrateful, indeed he would always bless brother John, as he did then, and as he did silently now in his grief, but the fact remained that the wicked "tow" shirt still had a good many scratches left in it after John returned it to him, weeks later.

Then came winter and the question of shoes. All around the quarters slave ingenuity went to work with the materials at hand. The results were strange to the eye: tops made of useless parts of hides fastened to wooden bottoms an inch thick. On hard walks or floors they created a fearful clatter and gave the wearers a peculiar stiff-legged stride, but Booker was still a little swollen with the pride his first pair instilled. A boy with shoes, he felt, was beginning to be a person.

Wearing shoes, and walking with a proper air, no doubt, he had been given his first assigned duty on the plantation. His task was to hold the reins of saddle horses while the riders were indoors or doing other things. Then he too was given a horse to ride, so that he could follow behind the ladies of the big house and their guests on their long horseback rides and be ready to scramble to the ground and hold their horses when they alighted. Booker recalled those experiences with a strange discomfort.

Perhaps it was the incident of the ginger cakes that embarrassed him. He had been holding the horses in the drive as the party of ladies stood on the veranda, tying their scarves and chatting, when suddenly their hostess, as a sort of afterthought, went into the house and returned with a plate of tempting ginger cakes, wonderfully odorous, and began passing them around. When they had eaten one round with obvious relish and many expressions of delight, the hostess passed the plate again. Then again. Booker's mouth watered. A mighty lust for ginger cakes tormented his stomach. What a life those women led, tittering among themselves and smacking their lips on ginger cake after ginger cake! He had felt a distinct envy.

Suddenly he had an ambition in life which changed everything. If only he could somehow put himself in the way of the ginger cakes, he would ask no more.

2.

Riding behind the ladies and holding their horses did not occupy all of Booker's time, however, and as the days passed he was put to a variety of small tasks, such as cleaning the yards and carrying water to the men and women in the fields. Eventually he was given a responsible errand. He was sent to mill with a sack of corn.

The trouble was that the mill was three miles away through forest and lonely country and the sack, containing three or four bushels of corn, was large and hard to cope with. When it was placed on the horse's back in such a manner as to let about half the corn hang on either side, Booker had an unpleasant apprehension of its becoming unbalanced up there with him on top, but there was nothing he could say as they hoisted him from the ground and gave the old horse a slap on the flanks.

Presently it happened in the forest as he had feared. A sudden lurch, a quick stop, and down the sack came with Booker on it. The road was deserted, and he could no more get the corn on the horse's back alone than he could fly.

Booker had been assured as a youngster that the woods around Hales Ford were creeping with deserters from one or the other armies at war and that deserters, as a matter of course, cut off the ears of the small colored boys they met. Waiting also consumed time, and Booker was old enough to know that the sun kept moving, no matter what, and that night would follow day.

Nor was he unfamiliar with the penalties exacted of slave people when the tasks with which they were charged did not go just right. Nothing in his memory remained so fresh and vivid as the spectacle of his own uncle, Jane's brother, stripped naked, tied to a tree, and whipped mercilessly in the sparkling, dewy morning. He could still hear his uncle's cries as the whip lashed his skin and wrapped around his body. "Pray, master! Pray, master!" Though Booker had not had a flogging yet, he knew there was danger as he waited beside the road.

Eventually someone came along and helped him get the sack on the horse and himself on the sack again, and the distressing errand was resumed. As he had feared, however, the time lost in the woods proved costly. Night fell before he was well started on the way home, and after the terrors of the black woods he was scolded and flogged on the plantation. Nevertheless he was sent again to the mill the next week, and in weeks that followed it became one of his assigned duties. Yet he continued to look forward to these journeys with dread.

Meanwhile other things were found for him to do. Occasionally he walked behind his young mistresses as they went to school, carrying their books to the schoolroom door. And once or twice he lingered outside after they had entered. The spectacle of white boys and girls reading books and writing on slates fascinated him. The folk around the slave quarters always talked about heaven. Booker promptly concluded that this must be it: youngsters no older than himself, sitting on benches, dressed in neat, well-starched clothes, looking into the eyes of their teacher and following his instructions.

Soon he found out why this privilege was denied to him and John and Amanda and the rest of the youngsters in the row of cabins called the quarters. Awakened before daylight one morning by the sound of his mother's voice, he suddenly began paying attention to the words of her prayer. Jane was asking God to bless President Lincoln and bring victory to his armies in the field so that she and her children could be set free.

So that was it. Slavery. Booker began listening more attentively to the whisperings of the old folks, and soon the names of Garrison and Douglass and Lovejoy and the rest began to have a certain meaning for him. He began to understand why the weekly or twice weekly report of the slave whose duty it was to fetch the master's mail from the post office was awaited so eagerly. This obsequious fellow, it seemed, would innocently linger about the place till he could get the drift of the conversation among the white people discussing the news. Returning home, he would often give the word to another slave who crouched behind a hedge or in a thicket, so that before he reached the big house, the quarters were likely to be buzzing with the latest battle report.

By the time Booker was given a job in the big house, he was indeed a little pitcher with big ears. His task, moreover, put him in a most favorable position to listen. In the big house of his master a system of paper fans had been constructed. These hung above the table in the dining room and were operated by a chord and a pulley. Booker was required in this way to fan the flies from the table during mealtimes. Naturally the conversations between the master and his family and their guests on the course of the war and its implications did not stop.

Instead of being oblivious to this kind of talk, as they imagined, Booker's mind recorded it, analyzed it, and waited for more. Between times he pondered with admiration the whole system of regular, organized meals observed at this table. No such practice existed in the quarters. Just a piece of bread here and a scrap of meat there was the way slaves were fed. If Jane had a cup of milk for him, Booker drank it on the spot. If she acquired a baked yam, she gave it to her young like a mother bird feeding her nestlings. Slaves were generally too hungry to wait for mealtime, and by the time Booker came along that fine old custom, the ritual of family or group eating, was little known among colored around Hales Ford.

While he fanned flies in the big house, the War went on and times grew more critical. The master's family complained of food shortages and other deprivations. Booker noticed that they seemed to suffer more under the hardship than did the slaves whose usual diet was corn bread and pork, both of which were raised on the plantation and continued to be available. The coffee, tea, and sugar which the master and his daughters missed so much were no loss to the slaves to whom they had never been available. But now the master was desperately trying to make coffee substitutes by parching grain and trying to sweeten the wretched drink with black molasses.

Young Booker took no pleasure in the miseries of these unhappy white people. By some quirk of nature, perhaps, this half-white son of the big-house cook, this unsmiling, honey-colored child who fanned the flies, seemed to take it for granted that as separate individuals they were not to blame for his condition or theirs. It never occurred to him to link their suffering with God's justice or any other form of cosmic retribution. At no time in those days or later did he allow himself the kind of cleansing hatred against his enslavers that nearly every other articulate slave expressed.

This attitude was not, of course, unique among the millions of slaves in the United States. It was simply unique among those with the capacity to think and feel deeply.

3.

Somewhere in the distance, meanwhile, the pace of marching armies quickened. Booker detected a fresh urgency in the whisperings of the older slaves. The folks in the big house contributed as much to the rumors as anybody. Trusted slaves were summoned hurriedly at midnight to bury the master's silver in the woods and then assigned to stand guard at the approaches. Every day or two, it seemed, another ragged deserter, unshaven and half-starved, appeared at Hales Ford.

Then the Yankee invasion began. Soldiers of the Grand Army fanned out over the countryside, demanding food, drink, and clothing, subsistence from the defeated land. They ransacked the slave quarters as thoroughly as they did the plantation mansions, and Booker was quick to note the divided loyalties of the Negroes to whom they brought the promise of deliverance. The slaves gladly surrendered whatever food or clothing they owned, but in no case did they disclose to the men in blue the secrets with which they had been entrusted by their masters. There was a point of honor involved.

But now the great day was approaching, and there was no longer need to suppress their true feelings. The singing in the quarters grew louder and bolder. It continued later into the night. More important, it began to include verses which expressed their ancient protest against slavery, their unbroken desire for emancipation. When they had sung these words before, they had been careful to point out to the master that the freedom for which they cried was the freedom of heaven and the world to come. Now the cat was out of the bag. The rabbit was in the brier patch. And everywhere slaves were exulting:

> *I can tell the world about this.*
> *I can tell the nation I'm blest.*
>
> *And he brought joy, joy, joy into my heart.*

Without missing a beat they glided into

> *Freedom, freedom, freedom.*
> *Freedom after me, after me.*
> *And before I'd be a slave*
> *I'd be buried in my grave*
> *And go home with my lord and be free.*

If a voice of caution rose, reminding them that the Confederacy was still fighting, they intoned,

> *Stay in the field,*
> *Stay in the field*
> *Till the war is ended.*

Before they could get the words out of their mouths, events moved to a climax. In the dark cabin in which Booker, John, and Amanda slept on the floor with their dark, tired mother, a rap was heard on the door. Sleepily Jane rose. All the slaves were being called to the big house early the next morning. Young and old were expected—everybody. When the door closed, Booker lay wide awake, every nerve in his body tingling.

Presently voices could be heard throughout the quarters. What was this? Booker did not sleep much that night, and he fancied that most of the other slaves slept as little. Then at daybreak he and his brother and sister followed Jane outdoors, where they joined a procession from the quarters to the veranda of the master's house. Nobody was boisterous or exultant now. Booker noticed expressions of uncertainty, deep interest, even traces of sadness on the faces of the older people.

Soon they were all standing before the veranda listening to a strange white man who made a speech and read from a paper. If the nine-year-old Booker heard any of the words of the Emancipation Proclamation, he certainly did not understand them. It was only afterwards that the thought was conveyed. The United States officer explained simply that they were now free, all free, free to go when or where they wished. With tears in her eyes Jane bent down and kissed each of her children.

While the slaves shouted and praised God, laughing and crying at the same time, Booker marked a subtle change in their mood as they returned to the quarters. In less time than it took to walk from the big house to their cabins the tremendous burden of freedom fell upon their minds and hearts. Where did a free man go—a free woman? What about food, a place to sleep, and the care of children? And the old folks, the decrepit ones seventy or eighty years old, whose hallelujahs had split the air so spontaneously when the Proclamation was read, what became of them now?

Within a few hours there was actual gloom in the quarters. Some slaves had even begun to think sympathetically of the old master and his family and to wonder how they would survive without the help of the people on whom they had depended all their lives. Now it became plain that a fondness between human beings often existed across the difficult, unnatural, and played-out relationship of master and slave, and as the evening of the first day of freedom fell, Booker caught glimpses of first one then another old slave slipping stealthily from shadow to shadow, making his way to the big house. Later he saw these reluctant freedmen cupping their hands as they whispered to their former owner, and he was convinced that they reached agreement. Between these parties there would be no separation, not immediately anyhow.

Another group of freedmen kicked up their heels and galloped away from Hales Ford like colts for whom the barn door had been opened. A few days later, while Jane and her three young ones lingered uncertainly on the plantation of James Burroughs, a certain number of these galloping ones returned, frightened by the responsibilities and risks of freedom, and made compacts with the master to carry on as before. Booker got the distinct impression, however, that these returning ones were in an awkward position for negotiating. He took note of the advantage enjoyed by those who had been less impetuous. Then suddenly a small wagon, drawn by a team of mules, appeared in the quarters and Booker's boyish observations of confused or embarrassed freedmen on the Burroughs' place were interrupted.

The wagon, its driver explained, had come from West Virginia. It had been sent by Washington Ferguson to fetch his wife Jane, his daughter Amanda, and his half-white stepsons John and Booker, and its arrival galvanized the cabin of the big-house cook and her brood. With John and Booker dashing wildly in and out of the hovel, carrying bags of stored corn, bits of clothing, the odds and ends of kitchenware that served for cooking and eating, the wagon was quickly loaded. A series of tearful little farewell scenes was enacted with Jane and the master, Jane and the mistress, Jane and their daughters, and Jane and her neighbors in the quarters as principals. Then Booker and the other youngsters climbed over the wheels and with their mother drove into the unknown.

4.

Weeks passed as the cart lumbered over the mountains of Virginia and West Virginia. Often the restless children ran alongside the mules or playfully ventured into roadside thickets. Meals were cooked over outdoor fires, and at night Jane gathered her young close beside her, and they slept under starlight. It was Booker's first journey, and now it seemed long ago and a part of another existence.

Recalling it from the past, he suddenly found himself shaking with fear. Something that happened back there had terrified him, something dreadful as he clung sleepily to the tired body of his mother. How could he ever forget it?

They had come to an abandoned house, not unlike the one in which John had found him tonight, and Jane had smiled as she explored and discovered that it was indeed unoccupied. In a few minutes she had logs burning in the fireplace and a pallet of rags spread on the floor. The room had just begun to feel cozy and safe under the pink glow of embers when the mother jumped up screaming, the terrified children clinging to her skirts. A black snake dropped from the chimney, twisted itself furiously on the edge of the fire and slithered across the floor. It was a long as a man.

Booker could not remember that they entered another "abandoned" house on that journey. Certainly Jane had wasted no time getting them out of that one, and they slept on the ground near the wagon as usual. Finally, the days and nights of travel having lost their identity, the family had reached Malden, a salt-mining suburb of West Virginia's Charleston, and there the vague Wash Ferguson had greeted the wife he had seen so seldom in slavery, the daughter he scarcely recognized, and the young stepsons who were strangers to him.

The house into which he led them, Booker remembered, had certainly been no better than the cabin from which they had been fetched. Moreover it was surrounded by other hovels which reminded the newcomers of the quarters on the plantation. But in other important ways Malden was totally unlike Hales Ford. Most of the shacks here were occupied by white people and not Negroes. To young Booker's surprise, these white people bore no resemblance to any white people he had previously known. They were blackened and dirty from working in mines, and they were as rough and boisterous in their talk as Negro field hands. The transparent air of the plantation was missing in this community. Instead, an umbrella of smoke from the mines hung above it.

When he ventured out to explore the new surroundings, Booker was shocked by the filth and the odors, the garbage on the ground, the stench of outhouses. When night fell and the men returned from the mines, he lent his ear, with horrified fascination, to their drunken talk, their lewd jokes, their gambling quarrels, their thunderous oaths, and their roaring fights. He noted with embarrassment their leering sex overtures, their bold seductions, their apparent shamelessness, and he slept eventually with a mind cluttered with sordid impressions.

But presently he had something else to think about. Wash Ferguson, it quickly developed, had plans for stepsons Booker and John. His hungering love for Jane, he now revealed, had not been his only, possibly not even his primary, motive in sending the mule cart to Hales Ford for the family. A few weeks in one of Malden's salt furnaces had given him ideas. A dull-witted man in some ways, he had not failed to learn at least one lesson in slavery: many hands make light work. Around him at Malden he saw white men with their whole families working in the furnaces and the mines. Strong boys had a distinct value, a value easily perceived by a stepfather with no special love for hard work himself and no sentimental feelings toward his dark wife's clear-eyed mulatto sons. Before Booker and John could get their bearings in the new community, he had them working beside him in a salt furnace.

What Wash had not counted on, perhaps, was that Booker's mind went to work at the same time that his hands became engaged in packing barrels of salt. The boy noticed that each salt-packer was given a number. Wash's was 18. At the close of the work day a boss came around and marked each of the barrels packed by Wash and his stepsons with these figures. Booker heard the number called. He saw the marks. Soon he could recognize an "18" and write an "18" as well as the boss. For him this marked the beginning of literacy.

Soon afterwards he begged his mother to get him a book—some kind of book. Where she came by it, or how, Booker never knew, but soon Jane surprised him with a copy of an old blue-back speller containing the alphabet as well as the simplest combinations of letters, and the young child laborer clasped it in his soiled hands with awe and affection. When he opened the book, however, the strange shapes and lines filled him with bewilderment. How could he read without an interpreter?

Not a single Negro known to Booker or Jane or their acquaintances knew how to read, but somehow or other, by compiling their hunches, no doubt, Booker worked out a part of the alphabet. There is no indication that he was a precocious scholar. Indeed the impression grows that he was a plodding learner where the book was concerned. Nor was he audacious enough, as the boy Fred Douglass had been, to wheedle from the white folks he met the secret keys to written and printed language. Booker's gifts were patience and watchfulness.

Months must have passed, as he recalled, before his wish was granted. Meanwhile there arrived in Malden a wandering colored youth from Ohio. The boy had been around town a good while before the other Negroes discovered that he knew how to read, and the revelation electrified them. Regularly thereafter someone would buy the newspaper and a group of eager freedmen would gather to listen as he read to them the latest happenings in the outside world. Booker was invariably in the group, less engaged by the events of the day than by the miracle of the boy reader, and his envy of the fellow's accomplishment grew by the hour. If he could only learn to read like that, he sighed, he would be satisfied, utterly satisfied with himself and his life.

Evidently other Negroes in Malden were thinking the same thing, for soon Booker heard the older ones talking about a

school for their children. The hitch, as they discussed it, was
the lack of a teacher. When someone proposed that the boy
from Ohio might do, the notion was dismissed on the grounds
that he was too young. Perhaps he also lacked the seriousness
desired by these people in a teacher, but the discussion continued unabated until another dark stranger from Ohio
showed up in Malden. This one, somewhat older, was named
William Davis. He was also a veteran of the Grand Army.
The discovery that he too could read and write instantly
resolved the troublesome question. The colored folks of Malden asked him to teach their children.

He would be paid as teacher, they agreed, by a small sub-
scription which each family would contribute monthly. And
since the salary thus collected would be too small to buy his
food, he would board around. That is to say, Davis would eat
and sleep one day with one family and the next with another.

If the plan did not look attractive in theory, it worked out
very well in practice, Booker remembered. The families vied
with each other in providing for the teacher. Indeed "teacher's
day" in Jane's household was eagerly anticipated by Booker
and John and Amanda. On no other day was the table so well
spread. It was the day on which the former big-house cook
called upon her best skills.

But the honor accorded the teacher was only partly based
on competition between the entertaining families. Among
people so starved for knowledge William Davis would have
cut a handsome figure under almost any conditions. Young
and old flocked to his classes, as Booker now knew they were
still doing all over the country, as he had more recently seen
them flocking to Hampton and seeking admission. Those who
could not leave work to be instructed by day insisted on night
school. The very old toddlers whose eyes had grown dim hur-

ried back and forth, busied themselves with the letters in the pathetic hope of learning to read the Bible before they died. Even the Sunday school turned into a spelling class, and like the day school and the night school, it was crowded thereafter.

The memory of that sudden, almost explosive, awakening in Malden was tinged with disappointment for Booker, however. Wash Ferguson took a dim view of all this agitation and shook his head decisively. He had not sent a mule cart all the way to Hales Ford to fetch a pair of yellow scamps who were no kin to him just to have them fritter away their time on book learning. He had brought Booker and John to Malden to work, and work they must. Booker was at his usual place in the salt furnace when the class began, and when he saw the other youngsters passing outside on their way to and from school, a great heaviness fell upon him.

It took him days to recover enough hope to consider ways to overcome the restriction Wash had imposed. Determined not to be completely outdone, he began studying his "blueback" speller again. He worked at it harder than before, and he began to feel that he was making some progress. Jane, who was in no position to oppose Wash's ruling, gave the boy such encouragement as she could, but their combined effort failed to satisfy Booker. Finally he made a bold proposal.

He asked the teacher to help him with his lessons at night. Tentatively, and perhaps not too eagerly, Davis agreed. If Booker felt like studying after work in the evenings, the teacher would take a little time to instruct him. That was as much as Booker wanted. Nervous and pent-up, his young mind snatched at every word the teacher offered, and for a time he was so thrilled by the adventure of learning that his long hours in the salt-furnace, his disappointment at not being permitted to attend school with the other youngsters seemed unimportant. From his teacher he got the impression that he was learning more at night than the other youngsters learned all day in school. Instead of making him content, however, this suggestion reawakened his eagerness to attend school in the regular way, and he began to express his desire again.

Eventually he got his stepfather to accept a compromise. Booker promised to be at the furnace early every morning and work till school time and then return after school and work two more hours if allowed to attend school for a few months. Caught off guard, no doubt, Wash grudgingly accepted the arrangement.

5.

Booker soon realized, however, that in his effort to be persuasive he had made promises hard to keep. The problem of working till nine o'clock and then being at school at nine o'clock, for example, was more than good intentions alone could solve, especially in view of the fact that the school was located a number of blocks from the furnace. Apart from the embarrassment of being tardy, with its customary penalties, Booker had the dismay of entering the schoolroom a few times after his class had recited.

He didn't like the strategem he devised to overcome this difficulty, but he convinced himself that it was justified under the circumstances. His eyes fastened upon the large clock in the office of the furnace, the clock which regulated the working hours of the hundred or more men in the plant, the clock which was the cause of his own immediate frustration. If that clock were half an hour faster than the clock which governed the opening of school, he reasoned, his troubles would vanish. That this would send the furnace crews to work ahead of time did not seem to him too serious, while the benefit to himself seemed enormous. Accordingly he began adjusting the hands of the clock each morning—and arriving at school on time.

But embarrassment is the daily bread of the new student, and Booker soon learned that entering the room late was not the only circumstance that could cause it. There was the matter of a hat or cap. The fact that he alone of all the boys in attendance had none made him uncomfortably conspicuous. His mother must have understood the feeling, for when he told her about it, she sympathized immediately. Of course, she had no money with which to buy him a "store hat," she explained, but since he was making such an earnest effort to get learning, she would have to see what she could do. A pair of old jeans provided the necessary cloth. By sewing two pieces together and then cutting to shape, Jane devised and constructed a headpiece that was at least wearable. Booker asked no more. His new cap filled him with pride. Now he was indeed a scholar.

Arriving at school on time and wearing a cap did not solve everything, however. There was the morning roll call. The teacher, Booker noticed, called each pupil by at least two names. Some youngsters even rated three. Booker's mind began to work fast, and when the time came for the teacher to add his name to the roll, he was ready.

"Booker Washington," he announced almost proudly, as if he had been so named from his birth. It had not yet dawned on Booker that names were acquired less casually in most instances. He knew that he had always been called Booker, that his mother had been called Jane, his brother and sister

John and Amanda. But now he was in school, and in school, he was quick to learn, you did as other pupils did. Conformity in his case involved naming himself on the spur of the moment.

In the years that had elapsed since those first school days, Booker could now recall, with amusement, the name of Washington had served him well enough. He saw no reason to hide its quaint origin nor to change it to Ferguson or Burroughs, either of which might have seemed to have some justification. Now Jane was dead, however, the link between Booker and his stepfather was broken, and of that the boy was not sorry. Neither Booker nor John respected the thriftless Wash Ferguson. Both had sensed a character deficiency that bothered them even more than his lack of skill as a workman. Wash was as self-indulgent and unfeeling as he was lazy. The link between Booker and the Burroughs' plantation, on the other hand, had been broken when the family moved to Malden, and that name had not even occurred to him as a possibility. No, Washington would do. Booker Taliaferro—

That was it. That was what his mother had called him. With Jane dead, the second name she had given him flashed through his thought again. Once or twice in his early childhood he had heard her say it, but then he had forgotten the word. He had heard it no more. Reminded of it again, he inserted Taliaferro between the Booker and the Washington.

The mournful little pageant moved again. The train of his thought, as he lay with his face on the rough floor, was as slow and retarded as a plantation burial in which the wooden coffin jogs along on a wagon and the field hands and their families follow it across furrowed land to the grave plot. Day school, Booker remembered, lasted only a short while. When the boss of the furnace realized that somebody was monkeying with the clock, Booker's school days were numbered. The boss promptly arranged to have the furance timepiece locked in a case, and once more Booker's attendance at his class grew irregular and then ended altogether. As Wash Ferguson demanded, he resumed full-time work in the salt furnace.

By now, however, Booker had quietly set his will against the man to whom his mother was married. His determination to learn became a passionate symbol. When he could not continue the night class arrangements with the regular teacher, he sought other people to teach him. He tried first one and then another. Generally a few nights was enough to reveal that the would-be teacher knew no more than the pupil and was hence of little value. To some of his evening lessons Booker had to walk several miles. But the distance, the physical exertion, were unimportant now.

Perhaps Wash felt, too, that this was a struggle between him and the boy. It had not continued very long before he arranged for Booker to be transferred from the salt furnace to a nearby coal mine. If an out-and-out declaration of hostility had been necessary, certainly this was it. Wash knew how the nervous Booker dreaded the coal mine. The face of the coal was at least a mile beyond the entrance to the mine, and to Booker this was a dark and dreadful mile indeed.

He had only to close his eyes to get lost again in the many "rooms," departments, and passages of the earth's bowels as he learned to know them there. And such blackness, such utter pitch blackness, would close about him now and then when for some reason or other his light went out! The horror of it had shattered his childhood. But not only was the mine dark and haunted. The work was backbreaking, and the place was downright dangerous. Blasts rumbled continuously. Again and again men or children were knocked out by falling slate or blown to kingdom come by premature explosions. In his fear Booker became aware of the unnatural state of mind these conditions induced in the individuals who had reconciled themselves to a lifetime of work in the mines. But here he was in Wash Ferguson's trap.

Would this have happened to him had he inherited a family name he could trace back two or three hundred years? Could a coal pit like this hold him if he were a white boy with no obstacles in the way of his becoming a congressman, a governor, a bishop, or even a president? Booker thought not. In the darkness below the earth he dreamed of success and traced in his mind the steps by which he might make his way to any one of these goals—had he been born of two white parents instead of just one. A feeling of envy for the lot of the white boys who worked beside him in the pit began to grow in Booker.

Even envy dies in a coal mine, however. A darkness of the mind settled upon Booker like the darkness of the eye that had seemed so fearful at first. Hope itself began to flicker wanly.

6.

How much time passed while he was working in the coal mine he would never know. Down there time was unimportant. Words spoken down there were as vague and empty as the talk one heard in a dream. Booker learned to ignore them too, but one day he could not help listening. Two Negroes were talking about a new school for colored people somewhere in Virginia.

At first Booker heard only snatches, but he felt himself

drawn toward the voices. Quietly inching nearer, he got the distinct impression that the school or college under discussion was to the little colored school in Malden as the sun is to a star. A moment later he heard words that yanked him out of his dull stupor. Not only was the school established especially for Negroes, the voices agreed, but in it opportunities were made for worthy students to work out part or all of their expenses. Trades and other means of self-support were taught them as they worked.

Was it then or later that he found out they were talking about the Hampton Normal and Agricultural Institute? Booker could not remember, and now it was beside the point. What was important was that he could think of nothing but Hampton thereafter, day or night, even though he continued to work in the coal mine. Months passed, months of painful toil in the underground darkness, but now despair was gone. Booker's mind remained active. His ears were always pealed.

So it was that he heard another rumor in the darkness. A job was open in the home of General Lewis Ruffner, owner of both the salt furnace and the coal mine in which Booker and his brother had worked with their stepfather. The position called for a chore boy to serve the General's finicky Yankee wife, but the word that went around in the pit was greeted with derision. Everybody but Booker seemed to know that the General's lady was an impossible person to work for. She was so unreasonable in her requirements she had seldom been able to keep a boy more than two or three weeks. Many of them were back in the mine—and happy to stay there rather than work for her. Indeed, her reputation as an employer was so bad, Booker did not even tell companions that he was willing to take a chance on the job as a means of deliverance from the mine. Instead he had asked his mother to apply for the job for him.

The salary was five dollars a month, and the arrangement provided for Booker to sleep in a small outbuilding only a few yards from the Ruffner kitchen. A shy boy of about fourteen, Booker had trembled as he approached the house on the bank of the river. He had trembled as the woman from Vermont sized him up with a cold skepticism born of a series of disappointments with slave-bred servants. He had trembled as she nodded and thumbed him to his new living quarters.

Instinctively he had begun to study this woman no house-boy could please. To his surprise, Booker had found nothing mysterious about her personality. Within a few weeks he had begun to feel at ease, knowing exactly what she expected—and demanded. Mrs. Viola Ruffner simply required that everything around her be kept clean and tidy. She insisted that her orders be carried out directly and systematically. Most important of all, she tolerated no fawning or dissimulation. Frankness and honesty were the fundamentals in her book. She would accept no excuse for a piece of stray paper in the yard, a picket off the fence, or finger marks on a door.

Once he learned to please Mrs. Ruffner, he had found, she had shown herself to be a far from inconsiderate person. Her attitude toward his ambition to learn had particularly surprised and delighted Booker, and when he discovered that she had no objection, he formed the habit of keeping a book handy for reading in a corner of the kitchen during spare moments. He acquired additional books and improvised a case for them from a dry-goods box. She encouraged his night study, whether it involved going to a lesson or keeping a light burning in his room till twelve or one o'clock.

She even let him have an occasional hour off during the day to drop into the school briefly, and for all these considerations Booker blessed her now, as he had then.

Had he been a rapid learner, the process might not have been so taxing or drawn out, but Booker had been from the start a slow student in figures, a quicker but not exceptional one in reading. Only in his speech had William Davis found the boy "easy and ready." In his present mood Booker himself was not inclined to question this estimate.

Mrs. Ruffner, he had discovered later, sympathized in a more general way with his desire to improve his condition. Several times when he heard of other job opportunities in Malden, she had allowed him to leave her employment without prejudice, and each time she had accepted him back after he found promise of the "better opportunities" to be an illusion. Of these the one Booker was most anxious to forget was a job he once accepted on a riverboat, but to Mrs. Ruffner it had only emphasized the boy's aspiration, and she had made it an occasion to reiterate her approval of anyone who wanted to "get on in the world."

The next day Booker had returned to the Ruffner kitchen garden, looking down on the river, filled his baskets with vegetables, as he had been accustomed to do, and gone out to peddle them at the furnaces down the stream.

On this bit of business the scene had faded, for soon thereafter Booker had announced his determination to go to Hampton. Then a few feverish days had elapsed as he made his preparations. It had been a bold, if not indeed a foolhardy, decision for Booker to make. He was practically without money, Wash having garnished his small earnings regularly. His brother John approved of the idea and was more than willing to contribute the change he had in his pockets, but John continued to earn very little in the coal mine, and most of that found its way into Wash's pocket. Despite the difficulties, however, Booker had let it be known that he proposed to let nothing stand in his way.

Gradually he had won a certain small measure of encouragement. Some of the older people began to slip nickles, dimes, and quarters into his hand. One or two made him presents of handkerchiefs as tokens. Booker had been touched by these gestures. He had seen in them evidence of an upward glance which long years of slavery had not succeeded in utterly destroying in these elderly folk. But it was his mother who had wrung his heart as he said his good-byes.

Why had he not noticed before that Jane was so weak and broken in health? While she had not wanted him to leave, neither had she tried too hard to prevent him. Her eyes had seemed more perplexed than hurt. Had he considered that this might turn out to be a wild-goose chase? Did he realize that he might never see her alive again?

Somehow or other his grave face had convinced her that he understood the perils, that he was ready to face them nevertheless.

And now Jane's story was concluded. It did not mark the end of Booker's childhood. He had left that behind when he headed for Hampton. His return to Malden was no more than a sentimental epilogue, but Jane, the dark woman whose blood was in his veins, into whose arms he sank dreamily in sleep when discouragments overwhelmed, Jane—

His brother's hand was on his shoulder again. Booker rose from the floor, and the two boys wavered out of the old deserted house like a pair of shadows.

7.

His thoughts still turning backwards, it now seemed to Booker that his sole reason for working and struggling to get an education had been Jane. His aim had been to ease her mind of trouble, her body of suffering. What other reason was there for the painful, uphill pull?

Weeks after Jane's burial Booker was still listening to his grief talk. The improvident Washington Ferguson, meanwhile, let things go to pot in the home. Unable to hire someone to cook for his children, he put the burden on the little girl Amanda. But Amanda was too young to keep house, and presently all was confusion where they lived. Sometimes there was a meal and sometimes there was none. Clothes went unwashed. The sweeping was forgotten, and the disorder sickened Booker. Two years at Hampton had unfitted him for a pigsty existence.

In his extremity he called on Mrs. Ruffner and told her how terrible he felt. The Yankee woman retained her favorable impression of Booker, though she had no regular job to offer, and she befriended him at her table as well as with words of encouragement. Eventually she found little odd tasks at which he could employ his time and earn small amounts of money, and this continued until Booker finally found work in another coal mine, somewhat removed from Malden.

By now most of the dreams with which he had begun his summer had faded. In relation to Hampton he was little better off than he had been before setting out two years ago. The hope of buying some new winter clothes for his third and last year of study at the Institute had of course been abandoned when Booker failed to find work in his first month at home, and now the question was whether he could scrape together enough money to get back at all. Grieving over his mother's death, he had been in a mood to forego even that, but down in the coal pit he began thinking of Hampton's lovely waterfront, of the classes filled with anxious students, of General Armstrong and other teachers he admired, and a new longing was awakened.

A few days later he received a letter. His hands blackened with coal dust, coal dust clinging to his sweaty eyelashes, Booker tore the envelope open. He was almost too excited to breathe when his eyes fell upon the signature of the lady principal who had put him through his qualifying assignment when first he presented himself at Hampton. Miss Mary F. Mackie was requesting Booker to return to Hampton two weeks ahead of time in order to help her clean the buildings and get them in shape for the opening of the fall term. Could he arrange to oblige her and General Armstrong in this way?

His heart leaping, Booker peeled off his dripping, gummy shirt and headed for the washbasin. The letter said two weeks before school opening. That left him another week, but when Booker checked his money and found that he had just about enough to pay his fare to Hampton, he decided to start immediately. Two weeks of work before the beginning of classes would put him ahead of the treasurer's office. By working as usual during schooltime, he could probably stay ahead.

Again John emptied his pockets of coins to help his young brother make the journey of nearly five hundred miles and as before shared with Booker such clothes as he possessed. And suddenly Booker's wan hopes began to revive. He hurriedly packed his little traveling bag, ran around Malden saying good-bye to the folks he counted as friends, shook the dust from his hat and coat, and headed for the train station.

III

A HAMPTON MAN

THE WAY Miss Mary Mackie washed windows, inside and out, cleaned woodwork, shifted mattresses, dusted furniture, and made beds was a revelation to Booker. He had known that Hampton teachers, including the lady principal, were not ashamed to work with their hands, but when Miss Mackie kept pace with him day after day, shirking none of the tasks she called on him to do, he was at first amazed and then puzzled.

That a New England woman of obvious culture, a member of an old and respected family, should plunge her hands into scrub water without a second thought, that she should not only be willing to wash second-floor windows, sitting in the panes, but also take pride in the work and seem pleased to be doing it was downright mysterious to Booker. Certainly that was not the way of the old South, of the planter aristocracy from which the ex-slaves had derived their notions of what was proper, and a basic difference in values began to penetrate the boy's mnid.

How important it was for the recently emancipated, he mused, to learn to work cheerfully and skillfully with their hands, to realize that such work is a blessing and a privilege, not a curse, that it does not detract from true refinement! How he would like to promulgate that idea!

But presently, classes began and competing interests were soon awakened. The foremost among these, where Hampton's better students were concerned in those days, was the honor roll of commencement speakers. Classroom excellence determined the selections, and somehow or other Booker had allowed himself to hope for this distinction in his senior year. So he buckled down to hard study, while continuing to work as a janitor to pay for his board.

The year slipped by quickly. In almost no time at all it was spring again. Small white-sailed craft appeared on the inland waterways around the Institute. The campus took on new green, and in chapel the honor roll was read and the names of the commencement speakers announced. First among these was the anxious but unsmiling Booker. He had made it! He was Booker Taliaferro Washington, and he could be what he wanted to be.

But he must not leave Hampton without first summing up his experience there. What had it all been worth? Booker thought long and hard before coming to the conclusion that two main benefits had been derived. He had met, associated with, and won the friendship of a near-perfect man, General Armstrong. That was the biggest thing and the best. What he had learned from books at Hampton had not been worthless, of course, and the coaching in public discourse under Miss Natalie Lord of Portland, Maine, had certainly done much for him, but he was in a mood to minimize all that. It was knowing the General that had changed his outlook. That, and the new attitude toward work which he had gained from Miss Mackie and the other teachers.

At the commencement exercises that year, before giving Booker his certificate, General Armstrong expressed the opinion that if Hampton had trained no other student in the seven years of its existence, the one now coming to the platform would justify all the costs and the sacrifices entailed by its founders. Whether or not the force of the remark was fully appreciated or its prophetic note detected in the excitement of the moment is doubtful, but Booker went out determined never to let the General down. His graduation picture was a study in clear-eyed intelligence, aspiration and will power, and the fact that he had no money with which to return to Malden and no prospects of a job of any kind apparently did not dismay him.

When school closed, someone came to the Institute to hire waiters for a summer hotel in Connecticut, and Booker snapped at the opportunity, without considering two small but pertinent details. He had never waited on table, and he had no money with which to pay train fare to the place of the job. The latter was solved when he succeeded in borrowing a little money. The matter of know-how he took more casually, and when he arrived at the hotel, he blandly presented himself to the man in charge as an experienced waiter and was promptly assigned to a table at which sat a group of people who looked terribly important.

But Booker's natural gifts did not include the ability to fake. At Hampton he had not learned to substitute glibness for knowledge, bluster for skill. His eyes were not right for even petty deception, and on the few occasions when he tried it, he made a mess. The important-looking people at the summer hotel in Connecticut called his bluff almost immediately. When he lost his nerve they became abusive. What kind of bumpkin was this? They had come here expecting deluxe service. They were paying good money. Booker quaked as he retreated backwards. Outside, he turned and ran, leaving them without food.

Instead of sending him back where he came from, the headwaiter compromised by reducing Booker from waiter to busboy. For several weeks thereafter Booker worked hard and penitently to regain his former status. When he finally made it, he could scarcely hide his joy. Achievement, especially achievement against odds or after a backset, delighted him to his very toes, and winning his credentials as a waiter, after his initial humiliation, sent him on his way with chin up.

But where would he go now? What would he do? Summer was past and the resort hotels were closed. Booker had money in his pocket and a certificate of graduation from Hampton Institute in his traveling bag. Should he return to Malden or try his luck in some other place?

Perhaps subconscious factors had more to do with his decision than the reasons in the front of his mind. Jane was dead, and without her the home kept by improvident Wash Ferguson for Amanda and John and a homeless boy named James, whom they had taken in before the mother's passing, was certainly not inviting. But Booker was attached to John. He missed his brother when he was away from home, and now another thought occurred. He was indebted to John. It was time he began considering ways to repay him for his help, for his sacrifices of money and for staying in the coal mine to help support the family while Booker went off to school. He loved Amanda too, and he was beginning to feel some responsibility toward her and the orphaned youngster James.

Moreover he had friends in Malden. He liked being in the

same town with such a woman as Mrs. Ruffner, and he was rather fond of the brusque old General, her husband, though he knew him less well. Yes, and there was a sweet-faced brown girl named Fannie Smith who lived beside a hill across the river. He liked being in the same town with her too, and a few days after leaving Connecticut he was there, stretching his legs on the hillsides and gazing across the twisting Kanawha.

2.

He had not been home long when he discovered that William Davis, the willowy, near-white Negro who had taught the little colored school since it first opened, would no longer be available as teacher. The subscribing families turned automatically to Booker. Hampton trained, starched and clean and of pleasing appearance, Booker was just what they wanted, and Booker, on the other hand, could not think of anything he would rather do at the moment.

He accepted the job. Promptly at eight o'clock each weekday morning he was in the doorway of the little one-room school with his handbell. He showed his pupils how to use a toothbrush, how to comb and brush their hair, and he extolled the virtues and pleasures of personal ablutions, good, soapy, washtub baths. Baths by the backyard water pump, baths in pool or river, baths under a waterfall or beside a cistern with somebody to dip and pour from a bucket were equally fine, for all baths were baptisms. They were holy.

To see how well they followed his instuctions he examined their hands and faces each day. He checked their clothing and noted buttons that needed replacement, holes that could be patched or repaired, as well as garments that needed washing. He gave as much stress to this side of education as to instruction in reading and writing and figures.

Which is not to say that Booker's pupils in Malden did not use their slates and blue-back spellers. They did. He kept them busy with books and pencils till school was dismissed. Then in the later afternoon and in the evening those who had to work days, as he had once been forced to do, came imploring afterhours instruction of the kind he had once received from William Davis. Remembering how he had been helped, Booker could not turn down any of this group.

They came in swarms, older boys and girls, men and women, some more than fifty years of age, many of them hopeless as learners, but all drawn by a feeling that there was something magic in education, something they could not afford to miss. In the face of the demand, Booker organized a regular night school with an enrollment about equal to that of the day school. He organized a debating society modeled after the one to which he had belonged at Hampton. And he got so wound up in these activities he was unable to suspend them over weekends. Sunday mornings he taught a Sunday school in the country, and Sunday afternoons he taught one in Malden.

Between times he taught his brother John his letters and began grooming him for Hampton. Soon he discovered other young people in town who had set their hearts on attending the school that had transformed Booker so miraculously. Each of these he encouraged and coached. No one who asked for private instruction was turned down, whether he could pay or not. Though he collected a small salary from Malden's public fund, Booker was not working for money. In a sense he was not working at all; he was having fun. He was on a binge. He had never dreamed such delirious joy was possible.

When he had saved a little money, he began repaying his debt to John in a more substantial way. With Booker's help the older boy was sent to Hampton. Meanwhile Amanda grew and became a more satisfactory housekeeper. Even with her whisky-drinking father upsetting chairs and sprawling across the beds with his shoes on, she managed to keep the place decent for her schoolteacher brother, for Booker transmitted to her the lessons he had learned in the dormitories and dining room at Hampton. Wash Ferguson, on the other hand, began to find these tidy precincts less and less inviting. Gradually he began to fade out of the lives of Booker and Amanda and young James, to vanish in an alcoholic mist.

Booker's first year of teaching drew to a close. Everything had been fine with him since he returned to Malden, but now it was June again and suddenly every muscle in his body went slack. The sun beat down on the little rustic school, and Booker felt a yawn coming on. Outside, the trees were green but motionless. Beyond there was marshy land and creek water. At intervals wings fluttered lazily, wings and the shadows of wings. Booker tried hard to keep his mind on the geography lesson to which the hour just before playtime was devoted, but the thought in his mind was that if he could just hold out till recess, he would forget to ring the bell when the time came, he would let the youngsters take double playtime, perhaps even more.

But the hands of the clock seemed stuck. The more Booker ran on about capes, peninsulas, islands, and lakes, the slower they moved. The more listless and bored his pupils seemed. The more stupid their answers to his questions. With one boy Booker almost lost his patience. The fellow could not even repeat definitions after the teacher, and

Booker began to wonder how anyone could be that stupid and live.

When finally he dismissed the room, there was a bolt toward the marshes. Within seconds, the liberated youngsters were leaping through the cool grass and splashing their feet in the water. Left behind, Booker felt himself irresistibly drawn in the same direction. Why shouldn't he? The inviting marsh, the soft grass, the still trees—why not? He pulled off his shoes, rolled up his pants, and bounded after them like a happy gazelle.

Up and down the water lanes they went, between the stumps of trees and over fallen branches, through floating leaves and around muddy bars. Presently Booker noticed that the boy whose dull listlessness had been hardest to penetrate in the classroom was the most eager and lively adventurer in the party. Was it a cape the teacher wanted to see, a peninsula, a lake, an island? Well he had them, plenty of them, and he promptly showed the other children how to find and identify them all along the edges of the marshy creek. Soon all the other youngsters were discovering miniature divisions of land and water.

The boy teacher's eyes brightened, his heart pounded with excitement. Here was something quite wonderful, Booker thought. As between the "study about things through the medium of books and studying things themselves without the medium of books," he mused, there was just no comparison. He would remember that in the future. It would be— well, one might say—the basis of his educational method.

But there was not much time for meditation. Booker had to splash to keep up with his exhilarated pupils. If this was June madness, he loved it. He forgot all about the bell that would normally have ended the play period.

3.

Booker's second year as schoolteacher at Malden was in many ways a repetition of the first. The round-the-clock teaching which never seemed to weary him or to grow monotonous, the recruiting for Hampton and the coaching of prospects, the debating society—all continued with unabated interest.

During these months Booker found himself enticed or badgered into another activity which turned out surprisingly well. Wrestling was a common sport in those parts. While their horses were feeding, farm boys wrestled behind barns. Men wrestled in front of the general stores. Boys, teachers, strangers, almost anybody was apt to get into a wrestling match on the school grounds, and the reluctant Booker was not exempted for long. Somewhat to his own amazement, no doubt, Booker discovered that he could hold his own in these contests.

With a few matches under his belt, in fact, he was able to do more than hold his own. He began to excel and to attract strong competition. Though his muscles did not bulge, his shoulders were not broad and his height was only medium, Booker suddenly realized that now he had attained his growth. He had become a man, and a right good one in a hard test. The feeling did him good. It also stimulated thought.

There was an embankment in Malden on which some of the wrestling matches were held. An odd place for a contest in one sense, it had a certain interest for spectators in that the winner was expected to leave his opponent at the bottom of the embankment. When Booker learned that it was much easier to wrestle a fellow to the bottom than to keep

him there, that to make sure he stayed put you had to stay
down there with him, a parable flashed into his mind, a parable of the black man and the white man in the Reconstruction South, a parable of subjugation or oppression wherever
it might occur.

Clearly the analogy had a context beyond the wrestling
fad in West Virginia. Nearly every newspaper brought dis-
quieting reports to Malden in Booker's second year of teaching. Lawless bands of hooded Klansmen swarmed over the
Southern regions. In their milder moods they flogged schoolteachers, black or white, to discourage efforts to educate the
emancipated Negroes, for they had not relinquished hope of
restoring slavery, possibly by terror. When aroused, they
burned homes and murdered the occupants. As a matter of
course, they defrauded Negroes of property and inheritance.
Booker read the news, listened to the talk, and turned the
parable of the wrestlers over in his mind. "You can't keep a
man in a ditch unless you stay down there with him," he
mused.

The ostensible motive of the Ku Klux Klan, Booker knew,
was stated in more innocuous terms. They aimed merely to
regulate the conduct of the newly freed Negroes of the
South; to people who remembered the patrollers of slavery
days, this was not too shocking. The patrollers had become
a familiar institution before the War. Composed of bands of
young white men with a property interest in slavery, they
rode the country lanes and pikes after nightfall to halt run-
aways. They broke up meetings of slaves which in their
judgment could lead to insurrection. They stood in the
shadows and behind thickets to catch bondsmen who ventured from one plantation to another without permission.

The Klan had started where the patrollers left off, but

even a child could see what they were actually up to. Their attacks on teachers and other innocent folk showed plainly that they meant to crush the spirit of freedom in Negroes, to break their will to sruggle and rise, so that they would lapse back into serfdom despite emancipation. And reading and hearing about them, Booker began to feel a strange uneasiness.

Then one night trouble broke in Malden. As usual in such situations the cause remained vague. Since everyone realized that the stated reason was unimportant, no one on the spot gave it a second thought. All Booker knew for sure was that a white mob made an attack upon the Negroes and that instead of scampering, as was expected, the Negroes of Malden fought the mob toe to toe in the streets. At the high point of the melee, Booker calculated that he saw close to a hundred persons engaged on each side. Naturally the opponents were not equally armed, and when the better weapons began to prove their value, there was a moment when it seemed that the fighting would end in a slaughter. It was at this moment that General Lewis Ruffner, husband of Booker's friend and former emyloyer, arrived. Rushing between the mob and its victims and throwing up his hands to restrain the attackers, the old soldier was promptly and ruthlessly slugged to the ground. The attack continued, but Booker staggered from the scene as if the blow had fallen on him.

In the following days, while General Ruffner lay critically injured, Booker began to ask himself questions. Was there any hope for his people in this murderous atmosphere? Was there anything that he could do as an individual? This teaching in which he was engaged—was it worthwhile under the circumstances? How about politics as a career?

When the school year ended in 1878, he was still without answers. The Ku Klux Klan, by its attack on the blithely unsuspecting Negroes of Malden, had rudely blasted the mountain idyl in which his dreams had reveled for two years. A black, despairing mood gradually overcame Booker's natural optimism. Even thoughts of Fannie, the brown girl from across the river, now attending Hampton, could not dispell the gloom, and when summer came and he knew he would not be able to stay in Malden any longer.

Surely there was wisdom somewhere, somewhere beyond the mountains around Malden. He thought of Washington, D.C., and suddenly the legendary figure of Frederick Douglass loomed in his imagination.

4.

Douglass was serving as Marshal of the District of Columbia when the Klan disorders occurred in Malden. He had begun the second year of his appointment and moved into the lofty mansion at Anacostia when young Booker was so cruelly awakened to the dilemma of his people. To Negroes in every nook and corner of the nation Douglass was an imposing man, to say the least. Sixty-one years old, excellent in health and bearing, heroic in stature, one of the most effective platform personalities America had produced, a brave veteran of the fight for freedom, and now a serene observer of the course of history, he would know, if anyone knew, the answers Booker sought.

It was not that the young teacher expected to meet or talk to the famous man, of course. While not unduly shy, Booker had an instinct for what was fit and proper, and he

did not have to be told that even as Hampton's most es-
teemed graduate to date, his education was nothing to flaunt.
He would go to Washington, but he would go there to study,
to observe, to learn. In the city of Fred Douglass, in the seat
of the federal government to whose Congress and Senate a
number of Negroes had recently been elected, he would
simply try to find his bearings.

Before he could get away from Malden, however, a wandering teacher applied for the job Booker was leaving. The
subscribing families were not impressed by the applicant's
handwriting, and this may have accounted for their decision
to examine his qualifications more closely. One of their questions had to do with the shape of the earth. How did he pro-
pose to instruct their children on it? To this he answered
glibly that he was ready to teach that the world was flat or
that it was round, depending on the preference of his em-
ployers.

As Booker listened to this, a childhood memory flashed
into his mind. The setting was the little Malden church
which he attended with his mother and brother and sister.
At the emotional peak of a moaning and shouting Baptist
service, with the preacher's voice soaring musically and the
flock quivering sweetly, a man had suddenly crashed in the
aisle. Booker remembered how surprised he had been that
no one rushed to help the poor fellow, that instead, the
shouting and the singing had grown more intense as he lay
there unconscious. Later, when the spell was definitely broken,
he had heard the bewildering explanation. The knocked-
out man had received a "call." Henceforth he would be a
preacher. But what if the man didn't want to be a preacher,
Booker had wondered. That too had been explained by his
elders. Having received the call, the man's own inclination

no longer mattered. He was compelled to be a preacher. And what if he was not capable of preaching? Don't worry. If he was called, he must be capable.

Booker remembered how a childish fear of receiving such a "call" had haunted his nights for several years thereafter, had in fact caused him to wonder whether or not he dared continue learning his letters, lest this achievement tempt whoever it was that gave the "calls." But now, his mind definitely set on going to Washington, he knew that the question of vocation was anything but childish or laughable. His people were pitifully mixed up, and he—well, he was no more able to guide them than he was to straighten out himself.

Located on Meridian Hill in the northwest of Washington, the school occupied a new four-story brick building, with accommodations for seventy-five students, recitation rooms, and rooms for faculty, and the boast of its teachers and students was that every brick in the structure had been laid by Negro workmen under the supervision of a former slave. It was operated by the Baptist Home Mission Society, and since 1865, the year of its founding, Wayland Seminary had been training teachers and preachers, primarily for work in Virginia and Maryland. Except that its students were Negroes, it had almost nothing in common with Hampton Institute.

But Booker had not come to Washington to find another Hampton. He had come to find his way in life, to get a perspective that three years at Hampton had failed to give. He had come to see and to ask questions.

Booker's classroom studies during the next eight months can be disregarded. If they made any impression on him at all, it was mainly to confirm his suspicion that the mastery of Latin and Greek had little value in the world in which he and most of his people lived. The street fighting in Malden remained too vivid in his memory. Though he performed his assignments in some fashion and even allowed politely that he had "derived a great deal of benefit" from them, the evidence was clear that his heart was not in his books. His first interest was his fellow students at Wayland.

Most of them were more sophisticated than the youth who had come to Hampton. They wore better clothes, jingled more money in their pockets, talked more wittily. In their classes they seemed brilliant by comparison. Many had come to the Seminary with the financial support of relatives or others. They were thus relieved of the necessity of toiling long hours for their board and keep, as was the custom at Hampton. Instead they enjoyed many hours of leisure.

The use many of them made of these hours appalled Booker. Sporting and posing, striking attitudes which reflected more interest in appearances than in reality, in shadow than in substance, they quickly convinced the young man from Malden that essentially they were a poor lot. They were unable or unwilling to do small but irksome tasks for themselves. When their money ran out, they wrote frantic letters to their families or patrons. When their allowances came, they splurged shamelessly, paraded through the streets of Washington like the children of millionaires.

In the face of such conduct their skill in languages, their smattering of philosophy, and their superficial familiarity with the fine arts struck Booker as sheer travesty, and he was outraged when they expressed themselves on the situation in the South. Go back there? Not if they could work in the North as pullman porters or as hotel waiters. Their readiness to turn their backs on the masses of Negroes still living

under the terrors of the Reconstruction was in marked contrast, he felt, to the prevailing attitude at Hampton where
it was taken for granted that graduates would return to the
communities from which they came and make themselves
useful, and he began telling himself mournfully that somewhere along the way these young people at Wayland and
those who fostered their education had missed the path.
They were lost, miserably lost.

5.

Nor was Booker encouraged by his first impressions of the
Negro community in the District of Columbia, but he drew
no hasty conclusions. Tirelessly exploring, he buttonholed
everybody he could stop, poked his nose into every open
door. He scrutinized housing, checked on employment,
wandered into the public schools, even examined the clothes
worn by the people he met. A natural-born social investigator, he began to correlate his data.

Many of the Negroes in Washington were fresh from the
South and had been drawn to the city either by lush accounts
of easy living there or assurances of the protection of the
law. A smaller, if in some cases more publicized, number had
come to accept minor government positions. These latter
were less numerous than still another group which had come
merely hoping for such employment. Among the newcomers,
as among the older Negro residents of the capital, Booker
found dramatic differences of education, economic circumstance, and social status.

A bright glamor surrounded the most highly favored personalities of the black community, and Booker had to admit they were doing right well. Some of the Negro members of the House of Representatives struck him as "very strong and brilliant" men. Blanche K. Bruce, Senator from Mississippi, inspired even greater admiration, while Douglass was a figure for veneration. Just below them in rank was "a large element of substantial, worthy citizens" with which Booker could find no serious fault, even in a debunking mood.

Still he could not help wondering a little. Was not the ground shaky under Senator Bruce and the lesser political figures? After a few months, when he saw men who had formerly been members of Congress out of office, unemployed, and in some cases in want, Booker felt that he had his answer. He began to question government service as a wise goal for the great bulk of the Negroes he saw in Washington straining every nerve in that direction.

He found himself gasping in alarm at the superficiality of the outlook which the general insecurity of life in this element of society seemed to produce. Young men who earned no more than four dollars a week thought nothing of spending half that amount to hire a buggy on Sunday to ride up and down Pennsylvania Avenue. Others who collected salaries of from seventy-five to one hundred dollars a month from the government remained in constant debt as a result of the outlandish standard of living they had adopted. Horrified by these, Booker switched his attention to the girls. All that Washington's excellent schools seemed to do for them was to create a taste for dresses, hats, shoes, and coats more expensive than their toiling mothers could buy, while at the same time making them unwilling to follow the menial occupations at which their mothers worked to send them to school, and the end of this spiral was certainly not pretty. The number who had gone to the bad seemed shockingly large.

Just what was wrong? Booker had no ready answer, but his hunch was that there was blame in several quarters. The federal government was probably the first and gravest offender, and in time he phrased his charge precisely. "It was cruelly wrong in the central government, at the beginning of our freedom, to fail to make some provision for the general education of our people in addition to what the states might do, so that the people would be the better prepared for the duties of citizenship."

The sins of the Southern states were obvious. Booker did not absolve them, but he preferred to focus his criticism on the shortcomings of the government in Washington and on the mistakes of his own people. Even the government's failure did not hide the fact that many of the freedmen who crowded the capital were looking for an easy solution to their problems, that they were not even using mother wit. Most of them should never have come out of the country, Booker reasoned. They should have remained on the soil "where all nations and races that have ever succeeded have gotten their start." Tedious and discouraging as life might be back there, it was the starting point. The good earth was the one great reality. They had gone astray when they left it.

While he investigated and pondered, months slipped by, and Booker grew restless again. He had come to Washington confused and upset, hoping that from this side of the Potomac he could see himself as well as the folks back home more clearly. Had it been worthwhile?

Of one thing he was sure. He would not remain longer in Washington. He would return to Malden and try again to make himself useful. Though nearly three years had elapsed, how he would start and what he would do were no easier to decide than when he returned from his summer in Connecticut after leaving Hampton, but Booker did not actually worry. He had staunch friends in the community in which he had grown up, and certainly there was an abundance of work to be done, work of every kind in the prostrate region to the south. He would go home and take his chances.

In Malden and in nearby Charleston the air was charged when he arrived, but this time the tenseness had nothing to do with Reconstruction disorders or the lawlessness of the Ku Klux Klan. The argument Booker heard as he made his way through the streets had to do with a proposal to move the capital of West Virginia from Wheeling, its current location, to some more central point in the state. It was not the kind of issue that a Southern Negro ordinarily got involved in, so Booker could smile and offer his good wishes to the local people who were pulling for Charleston, without letting the matter trouble his sleep.

To his surprise, however, some white people in Charleston had other notions. He had scarcely unpacked his bag when a committee visited him. They had not forgotten the boy teacher of the colored school in Malden. They remembered speeches he had made around town, even in some of their churches, when first he returned from Hampton. They had him down as a natural-born public speaker, and right now a natural speaker was just what they needed to canvas the state and help swing the referendum to Charleston, among the three competing cities, as the new capital.

When they finished talking, Booker nodded. He had not opened his mouth, but if that was what they wanted, he was at their disposal.

6.

Booker began touring the state, making speeches in public parks, in churches, at barbecues, on the steps of courthouses, wherever he could wangle a hearing, and as the time for the showdown approached, excitement increased. Newspaper editorials became more spirited, the headlines bolder, and the size and number of Booker's audiences grew proportionately. With him the campaign was a game only slightly more serious than the programs of the debating society at Hampton, but it offered wonderful practice in the art of persuasive talk before assorted crowds of people, and he made the most of the opportunity. He studied his performance from night to night, tried out different stories for their effects, gave attention to tempo, to pauses, and all the other devices for winning and holding attention. The tour was a three-month lark. Booker was thrilled.

The outcome of the actual vote did not take his breath, but he was calmly gratified when the count revealed that Charleston had won the referendum and the right to become the captial of West Virginia. The fact that his own speeches in behalf of the winning city were given due recognition also pleased him, but when local friends suggested that this might be a favorable time to launch him on a political career, he suddenly fell into serious thought. All the things he had seen and heard and mulled over in Washington came back with a rush.

While he hemmed and hawed and tried to make up his

mind, a letter came from General Armstrong at Hampton. His former teachers had heard about his speaking in connection with the referendum, and the General wished to invite Booker to return to his alma mater at commencement time to deliver "the postgraduate address," an honor accorded annually to a former student who appeared to be making headway.

Hampton seemed more beautiful than ever. There were handsome new buildings. During his absence the trees had grown. More important, the school had added more and more industrial training to its program. As the General explained, Hampton Institute was trying to meet the actual needs of its students. Each year experience strengthened his resolve not to be bound by traditional practices that had lost their educational point. To this line of reasoning Booker's mind vibrated like a plucked violin string. His admiration for Armstrong soared.

Perhaps it was this exhilaration that gave his commencement day address on "The Force That Wins" its special spark. On the other hand, the inspiration could have come from the serious, upturned face of Olivia A. Davidson, a member of the class of 1879, or from the equally rapt attention of his brother John, who was also among the thirty-nine proud graduates. But whatever the cause, the speech stirred the audience, and for the remaining hours of his stay on the campus Booker sat high and erect on a wave. He returned to Malden the same way.

Now he could see about getting his teaching job back again and begin once more to single out the brightest students for special coaching, preparatory to entering them in Hampton. What better career could he elect? To those who kept whispering that he was cut out for politics, he could

say no emphatically. Why suppose he should run for office
and be elected, or what was more likely at the moment,
work for the election of another candidate—what then? He
had seen with his own eyes a former holder of high office
working as a brickmason's assistant. But even if he were to
succeed where others failed, was there not a ceiling above
which he as a Negro could not hope to rise? Booker sensed
a certain naked exposure in the position of the Negroes he
had seen holding office. He compared them to tennis balls
batted back and forth by Republicans and Democrats.

He had been home only a few weeks when another letter
came from General Armstrong. Hampton wanted Booker
back again in the fall, and to his surprise the invitation was
not based on his delivery of the postgraduate oration. The
General and his teachers had been evaluating their former
student by less spectacular evidence. In the two years of his
teaching Booker had returned four of his pupils to Hampton,
not counting his brother John. These had all been so well
instructed that they had been placed in the "advanced" class
when they entered the Institute. Moreover, others were
ready to come in the fall, among them James, the adopted
boy in Booker's family. These were the things General Armstrong and his staff had in mind as they considered Booker
for a new project they were about to introduce at Hampton.

One of the General's unconventional notions was that
American Indians, as well as emancipated Negroes, were
able to benefit by the kind of education his father had suc-
cessfully developed for the natives of the Hawaiian Islands
and which he had in turn introduced at Hampton. Despite
widespread skepticism, he had proposed a full-scale experiment to test his new theory at the Institute. He had gone so
far, in fact, as to make arrangements with reservations in the

Western states for delivery of more than a hundred so-called "wild Indians" at Hampton almost immediately. Booker's role in the General's enterprise was that of preceptor or "house father" to the young red men. Would he accept the job?

Booker did not jump at it. Elementary teaching and the other activities he had outlined for himself in West Virginia suddenly began to seem unusually attractive, but perhaps nervousness about the unusual assignment was the main factor. Any offer from Hampton was a glorious prize, however, and presently Booker reached the conclusion that even this one could not be turned down.

So it was back to Hampton again at the end of the summer of 1879, a journey which by now had become so familiar that Booker almost knew the turns by heart.

7.

A member of the Institute's regular staff, Booker took up residence in a dormitory with about seventy-five Indian "boys," many of them older than himself, and immediately his knees began to quake. Fortunately no fear or uncertainty showed on his face or in his voice, for the Indians let him know that they considered themselves better than white people and far better than Negroes. The latter attitude, Booker gathered, was based on a casual assumption that the Negro had submitted to slavery while the Indian had refused to submit. In fact, the Indians had enslaved a good many Negroes themselves in the Indian Territory from which many of Booker's charges came.

The young braves behaved more like prisoners of war than students. Booker could see their profound distrust of the whole operation, and he set his mind to penetrate the unsmiling enigma with which he was confronted. The young Indians grew mutinous when compelled to have their long hair cut. They angrily resisted demands that they exchange their blankets for the pants and shirts worn by Hampton students and teachers, and they were ready to fight rather than give up smoking their pipes. Nor were they responsive to the religion promulgated by those into whose hands they had been delivered.

Despite the barrier of language, Booker did not find it too hard to discover a certain logic in their behavior. The Indian's idea of civilization, he observed, was not the same as the white American's. That was the problem in a nutshell. They were not convinced that their way of life was inferior. Even the benevolent and understanding white teachers at Hampton found this a little hard to understand, but Booker quickly saw both sides and began drawing some conclusions about human nature. The Indians were simply like other people, and like other people, he calculated, they would respond to honest dealings, to kind treatment, to mutual respect. At least that would be his approach to the dormitory situation in which he found himself.

That it worked was, of course, not surprising. Within a few weeks the seventy-five young Indians were solidly with him. Nothing they could plan or contrive was too good for Booker. They seemed always preoccupied with his comfort and pleasure. He had shown them that he was on their side, and they let him know in a score of ways that they were on his. It was no longer hard for Booker to supervise their education.

The rapport between him and the Indian students was followed by growing friendliness between the Indians and the Negroes on the campus. At first the Negroes had been anything but cordial, for their first thought was that every Indian student admitted to the Institute took the place of a Negro who might have otherwise come to Hampton, but this attitude soon faded. When someone suggested that a simple way to deal with the language difficulty of the Indians might be to give them Negro roommates, the Negro students readily agreed. By this time the success of the experiment as a whole was assured, even from the point of view of Hampton's missionary faculty. By living in close touch with Negroes, the Indians eventually began to discard their blankets, to trim their hair, to show some regard for Hampton's ban on smoking, at least in public, and otherwise adopt the civilization they had at first rejected, while at the same time making some headway at acquiring the trades and vocational skills offered at the Institute.

But the climax of Booker's year with the Indian students occurred away from the Institute. In the course of the crowded year, rising early in the morning, studying late into the night, hurrying back and forth across the campus at the ringing of bells, sitting rigidly at attention in chapel and at other gatherings, marching to the dining hall and eating on signal, one of the young braves fell ill. The strain of the new routine and the awkward, sometimes painful, adjustment had somehow overtaxed a body conditioned to desert suns, to horsemanship, and the freedom of open spaces. As his fever rose, the folks at Hampton decided there was only one thing to be done. The Indian boy must be dispatched to the Secretary of the Interior for return to his reservation.

Booker was given the assignment, and he and the young Indian were driven to Old Point Comfort where they boarded a steamboat for Washington. A few hours passed while he and his sick charge sat quietly in the stern of the vessel or stood at the rail to stretch their legs. When the bell rang for dinner, Booker was hungry but he decided to wait till after the first rush. Finally he and the Indian boy went to the dining room. Seeing them, the steward's brow clouded. Booker knew that facial expression, but he was not sure what the attitude would be toward serving the Indian or how the steward would classify him under the circumstances, since the sick boy was actually a little darker than Booker. By special intuition, however, the steward decided that one was an Indian and the other a Negro, for he politely informed Booker that the Indian might eat, but that he might not.

The experience on the steamboat was still in his mind when Booker entered the hotel in Washington to which he had been directed. Without a moment's hesitation the clerk at the desk announced that he would be glad to give the Indian a room but that Booker could not be accommodated. Both incidents made indelible impressions on Booker's mind, but he was more intrigued than angered. Surely something more than pure cussedness was at work here. Was it an illness of some kind? Booker recalled other instances of the enforcement of Jim Crow customs, some ludicrous, like the time when a railroad conductor seriously examined the feet of a light skinned man for a clue to racial identity not otherwise apparent, some unbelievably cruel, and he recognized a kind of coarse humor in what the gods had done to the Southern white man to make such an outlandish practice seem essential to his peace of mind. Though his face remained grave, Booker smiled inwardly. Presently a roar of inner laughter brought him to his feet. Was it the beginning of wisdom?

The next day he took the slender, fever-racked Indian to an office in the Department of the Interior and received for him a receipt such as one might get for the delivery of a package.

8.

At the beginning of Booker's second year of employment at Hampton, General Armstrong had another brainstorm. Though the Institute had now been in operation for more than twelve years, there had been no noticeable reduction in the number of penniless students, generally wholly illiterate, who came begging for admission. Though General Armstrong and his associates, together with their friends and supporters in the North, worked constantly to increase the number of scholarships and extend opportunities for education in every way possible, they were still not satisfied with the results. Crowds of eager but otherwise unpromising young Negroes still besieged their gates, and the nightmare that troubled their sleep was that among those they were forced to turn away there might be another Booker T. Washington. How could they ever be sure when they were unable to offer all a chance to prove themselves?

Well, the General had a plan. He had ascertained that Hampton's farm and its carpenter shop and other industries could profitably use more hands, and it occurred to him that students sincerely anxious to secure an education might be willing to work ten hours a day for the Institute without wages on condition that they receive room and board and be permitted a couple of hours of instruction evenings, on the one hand, and that at the same time credit be built up for them in the business office so that after two years of this they could begin regular daytime classes.

Booker was the person to teach this class of students, General Armstrong stated, after outlining the plan, and the words were scarcely out of his mouth when Booker went to work. Twelve students were enrolled immediately, the young men working in the school's sawmill by day, the young women in the laundry, and Booker began to teach them with so much enthusiasm that the word began to get around that this was not a bad bunch at all. In fact, their morale was so good, Booker had trouble disbanding them when the lights-out bell rang on the campus. They did not want to break up their study sessions. Others heard about the project and applied for admission on the same basis. Within a few weeks the enrollment had more than doubled.

The eagerness and industry of his students almost embarrassed Booker at first. What could he give them in recognition of their effort and their progress in learning? Something important had been overlooked in the General's plans. Booker decided to supply it on his own authority. He went to the printshop and had a quantity of handsome certificates run off with wording which he thought might serve the purpose: "This is to certify that............is a member of the Plucky Class of the Hampton Institute, and is in good and regular standing." After a student had been in the class for a reasonable time, he became eligible for one of the certificates.

The Plucky Class displayed these emblems with great pride, and enrollment in the night school continued to swell. It was still flourishing when another spring colored the hedges and slopes of the campus. Booker was pleased with his work. His first year's occupation with the Indians had been interesting enough, but the Plucky Class had given

him a real thrill, and anyone could see that another Armstrong experiment had justified itself, that the night school
was at Hampton to stay. Booker found himself walking a
great deal, early mornings and at nightfall. The inland waters
around the Institute, the green world, the burst of spring,
the Plucky Class—it was all stimulating. All good. Then why
was it that every now and then a strange loneliness suddenly
fell upon him?

He had no gift for poetry, the proper expression for such
experiences and sentiments, and hence was more than normally tongue-tied. In his public addresses he seldom if ever
quoted verse. Nor was a sense of rhythm one of Booker's
endowments. At twenty-three he had not learned to dance.
No one ever heard him sing. He had never had the time or
inclination to try his hand at a musical instrument. Even
his reading in fiction was noticeably limited. Though he continued to study and read privately with Reverend H. B. Frissell and other Hampton instructors, only Dickens interested
him among the novelists of the day, and that interest was
probably more sociological than aesthetic. He had been introduced to Shakespeare and the Bible and was now cultivating the habit of reading them as a sort of intellectual ritual,
but neither became a part of his own self-expression, except
perhaps in the matter of parables. He never quoted from
either directly or indicated that his own strings vibrated to
their sweet music.

His was in nearly every sense a world of cold reality. Yet
something powerfully urgent was stirring inside him as
Booker reached his vague twenty-fourth birthday and the
school year of 1879–80 drew to a close at Hampton, and it
was not interrupted seriously until one evening General
Armstrong surprised the student body and faculty by read-

ing a letter he had just received. The chapel exercises were over, and a sort of calm had settled, but before they returned to their rooms, he thought it would give them pride to know that some gentlemen in Alabama had been sufficiently impressed by the work at Hampton Institute in Virginia to ask the General if he could recommend someone, someone like himself presumably, to take charge of a proposed normal school in Alabama for Negroes in that state.

To Booker the tone of the letter was warmly gratifying, reflecting as it did approval of General Armstrong's work, approval which many southern people hesitated to give, and indicating a respect for the General's endorsement of people. Clearly the men in Alabama had in mind another white man of the General's stamp who was prepared to sweat blood in Alabama as Armstrong had done at Hampton, and Booker went to his room in the Indian dormitory encouraged by this straw in the wind of public opinion. Surely the South needed more schools comparable to Hampton, and from what he had heard, nowhere more than in Alabama. What was the name of the town from which the letter had been addressed? Was it Tuskegee? Well, something of the sort—an Indian-sounding word, as near as Booker could make out. Certainly it was not a name he had ever heard before, and by the next morning Booker had forgotten it and more or less forgotten about the letter from there.

But General Armstrong had something else in mind, and during the course of the day he called Booker to his office. Could Booker guess why he had been summoned? He could not. Well it was about that letter. Booker's eyes twinkled humorously, his usual substitute for a smile. What Armstrong wanted to know was whether or not Booker thought he could fill the position described in the letter from Tus-

An early portrait of Booker T. Washington

Washington as a young man with a moustache

Fannie Smith Washington (1860-1884), first wife of Booker

Washington with his third wife and family: left to right, Ernest Davidson, Booker T., Jr., Margaret Murray Washington, Portia Pittman

Washington on his favorite horse, Dexter

Washington as a rising young educator

On a speaking tour of Alabama

Washington with unidentified officials of the National Negro Business League, which he founded

Washington, the founder of Tuskegee Institute

Washington in his garden at Tuskegee Institute

Booker T. Washington in
1906

Sons Booker T. Jr. (center)
and Ernest Davidson (right),
ride with their father

Washington with his secretary, Emmett J. Scott

Washington with officers and members of the National Negro Business League and Farmers' Association at Tuskegee Institute

Margaret James Murray Washington (1865-1925), third wife of Booker

One of the last photographs of Booker T. Washington, taken at Shreveport, Louisiana, October 15, 1915

kegee. The twinkle faded as Booker caught the full force of the General's question. After only a slight pause he nodded. He would be willing to try, he said.

That was what General Armstrong had hoped he would say, for it happened that he did not know another white man whom he could recommend who was ready to undertake such an assignment. He would have to say that in his reply, but he had thought of adding that if they would accept a Negro teacher, he would recommend Booker T. Washington, a graduate of Hampton now connected with the Institute's staff. Booker assured him that that was agreeable to him, and on that note he left the principal's office.

He never remembered how many days elapsed before further word was received from the correspondents in Alabama, for neither he nor the General had any assurance that the substitute suggestion would be welcomed, and Booker was sensible enough not to arouse his own hopes prematurely. Meanwhile, however, the other teachers at the Institute were told what General Armstrong had written, and word trickled down to the students. Just what this amounted to as an opportunity for Booker was not too clear, but his popularity was such that the whole campus found itself pulling for him. If it was to fill the shoes of a man of the General's stamp, it must have been important. They were backing Booker solidly.

The Sunday evening chapel exercises, as a result, seemed to have more than the usual seriousness. There was the usual singing, followed by the prayers and the heart-to-heart talk by the principal. General Armstrong, erect and silvered, the soldier of freedom, crusader for the education of freedmen, in Booker's eyes a knight in armor, was discoursing with his usual calm effectiveness when the quiet lamplit meeting was suddenly interrupted. A messenger from the town of Hampton entered, walked to the platform, and handed the speaker a telegram. The General paused, opened it, and a moment later read to the audience: "Booker T. Washington will suit us. Send him at once."

The next morning, still a trifle giddy with excitement, Booker slipped away from the groups of students and teachers who waited in every hallway and under every tree to congratulate him. He went to the library and began searching on maps and in atlases and geographies for the unheard-of place called Tuskegee. But in none of them could he find it, either in bold print or small.

What if Tuskegee did not exist? What if there was no such place in Alabama. Could the whole thing have been a hoax?

I V

TUSKEGEE

MEANWHILE, in Macon County, Alabama, a Negro citizen struck a bargain with a small-time politician.

A man of intelligence, Lewis Adams had learned to read and write as a slave through the forebearance of his white father. He had also acquired competence as a cobbler, a harness maker, and a tinsmith on the plantation. All of these skills came in handy after emancipation, and Adams proceeded to make the most of his opportunities. He opened a shop.

Business was good, and Adams did not neglect his customers, but it was not long before folks around Tuskegee began to see and draw upon still other abilities possessed by the versatile craftsman. He became a leader in the Methodist Church, where respect was shown for his opinions. Sometimes he talked politics under a tree and encouraged the newly enfranchised voters to support the Republican ticket, for the Reconstruction had not entirely missed them, even in their remote and peaceful community. In 1874, when Booker was beginning his last year as a student at Hampton, Adams went down to Montgomery as a representative to a Republican Negro convention. But in 1880 he was buttonholed by a Democrat.

Colonel W. F. Foster, a veteran of the Confederate Army, a former slaveholder and now editor and publisher of *The Macon Mail*, a local newspaper, had set his eye on a seat in the Alabama Legislature. Considering the number of Negro voters in the area and the fact that most of them were still under the spell of their Emancipator, and the party with which he was identified, Foster did not figure to win under normal circumstances. He saw no reason why he should not make a forthright effort to swing some of the Negroes to his side, however, and it was for this purpose that he approached Lewis Adams.

Adams did not hedge. A large man and a straight talker, he told Colonel Foster that the thing his people needed most in Tuskegee was a normal school. Nothing pretentious, just a place for the training of teachers to staff the poor cabin schools in the outlying districts. That was what the Negroes talked about most, and if the Colonel could see his way clear to introduce and support the necessary legislation in the state Senate, Adams was convinced that such a pledge would result in a good many votes in the next election.

To Colonel Foster this seemed fair enough, despite considerable opposition from whites who feared that education would spoil Negroes as servants. Arthur L. Brooks, running for election to the lower house, when he heard what was up, responded favorably to a similar suggestion.

Whether or not the parties to the agreement fully trusted each other at the time is not too clear, but they might have, for both were men of honor. Colonel Foster went to the Alabama state Senate with the help of Negro votes and promptly introduced a bill such as Lewis Adams had requested. He then put up a successful fight for it on the floor. But his colleagues in the state Senate appear to have been in a playful mood when they eventually let it go through. In its final form, as approved on February 12, 1881, the bill merely appropriated two thousand dollars, from the fund for public education, to pay salaries for the staff of "a normal school for colored teachers at Tuskegee." Nothing about a building or other essentials was even mentioned. The bill did, however, name three commissioners to administer the appropriation, and one of these, significantly, was Lewis Adams of Tuskegee, whose idea it was originally.

Of the two other commissioners only one became important to Booker Washington, and this one not intentionally. This man, seriously ill at the time of his appointment, was in no condition to consult with Adams about steps to implement the action of the Legislature. The third commissioner, "a scholarly gentleman," did not even live nearby. So there followed a short period in which it seemed that nothing would come of the bargain struck by Lewis Adams on behalf of the Negro voters and their new state senator.

Strangely, the first expression of impatience about the delay came from a completely different source. George W. Campbell, a white storekeeper and town banker in Tuskegee, called the situation to the governor's attention, and when the sick man on the commission died, it was Campbell who was appointed to fill his place. This appointment provided a basis for action, for Campbell and Adams, ex-slaveholder and ex-slave, put their heads together and dictated to Campbell's son the letter and telegram to General Armstrong at Hampton, which both of them signed.

There is a legend at Tuskegee which says that before corresponding with Armstrong, the two men were in touch with

Fisk University, Atlanta University, and Talladega College, from whom they sought names of teachers willing to come and start the school, and that one of these sources named a white man who actually arrived in Tuskegee that spring. When this vague character discovered that the school he had been invited to direct did not exist, that it had in fact neither land nor building, nor teachers nor students, he gingerly brushed the dust from his trouser legs and vanished.

Booker might have vanished too, given half a chance, but when he climbed out of the little omnibus that connected with the train at Chehaw and brought him the last five miles of the way to Tuskegee, he knew instinctively that it would not be that easy. His suitcase beside him on the road, his paper collar wilted, he looked in one direction and then the other. Finally he started walking.

2.

Lewis Adams' home, in which Booker found lodging, was less impressive than his shop on the square. In fact, it seemed ready to collapse. Located on South Side Street about a quarter of a mile west of the square, its main advantages were a pump and washbasin near the back door and a tub for boiling water in the yard. That was a comfort. Even so, Booker could not sit still. Until he could get out on the street again, he remained as tense and nervous as a cat.

The little town seemed friendly. The trees, the layout of the buildings and houses reminded him faintly of Connecticut villages he had seen. But what about the school he was to teach? Where was it?

Lewis Adams broke the news as gently as he could, walking back to his shop, but he did not have to be told that young Booker's clear grayish eyes would accept only the unvarnished truth. There was something about the new teacher's immobile features, his penetrating gaze, his boyish mustache that discouraged any inclination to pretend. The situation was only slightly better than Booker had guessed by this time. There was no school.

On the other hand, there *was* the appropriation and the authorization by the Legislature. Yes, and there was the need for such a school as had been authorized. All through the country for miles around the need was painfully apparent. The people were ready. They were eager. The cooperation of the white people in the community was also assured. Adams and George W. Campbell, the two local commissioners, saw eye to eye on this project. They were prepared to give the proposed school the best support they could.

Presently Booker got a hint of what must have been in Lewis Adams' mind with respect to cooperation between whites and Negroes. In the hardware store he noticed a Negro clerk and a white man both serving customers. About this he had to ask. He learned, to his amazement, that the two were partners, joint owners of the business, the only hardware store in town. But neither white people nor Negroes seemed to think this strange. It was typical of the general attitude in Tuskegee. On the surface, at least, there were no racial tensions, no neurotic fears. Booker began to feel that he was going to like the place.

Perhaps the explanation was in the people themselves, he reasoned. While the Negroes he saw seemed no further advanced educationally or economically than others he had known, Booker felt that they were in a healthier state of mind and body than the freedmen who flocked to the big cities after emancipation. These in Tuskegee appeared to have picked up fewer vices. They were good material.

Of course he was desperately anxious to see something hopeful or encouraging, now that he was here, now that all eyes at Hampton were focused on him, and now that Fanny Smith was expecting him to come back and get her next year, but he seriously believed he was not being unrealistic about the human resources he observed. The black folk were wholesome peasants, and the whites were certainly not trash. While the latter could not be called aristocrats by antebellum definition, they did possess a kind of quality which in Booker's book connoted decency in racial attitudes as in other matters.

George W. Campbell, the town banker, did his best to confirm that impression. He could recall with pride that during slavery the area around Tuskegee had been regarded as a center for the education of white people, thanks to the presence of such institutions as the East Alabama College (Baptist), the Alabama Conference College (Methodist), and the East Alabama Female College in Tuskegee and the East Alabama Male College in nearby Auburn. That tradition persisted, he thought. Booker and the white commissioner agreed. They hit it off well togther.

Booker was particularly interested in what Campbell knew about the history of the town. Having been brought there by his parents in 1835, just two years after the main streets were laid out, Campbell had literally grown up with Tuskegee. If Booker wanted to know why the main line of the Montgomery and West Point Railroad came no nearer than Chehaw, the point at which Booker had transferred to the omnibus on arriving, if he was interested in the building of the courthouse on the public square or the events leading to the establishment of the principal businesses, Campbell was able to inform him. He was also able, Booker gathered, to speak about the individual citizens of the town in fairly specific terms.

Campbell knew most of the people intimately. He remembered that before 1860 they had been prosperous farmers, that their crops of corn, cotton, peas, and potatoes had generally been good. Their plantations had been efficiently administered. There had been fish in the creeks, in those halcyon days, birds and wild game in the pinewoods. Peaceful slaves worked the fields, drove the oxcarts, cut the wood, and polished the silverware. A short spur line connected the town with the main railroad. Then war had come. With the disorganization of the working force, the economy had been wrecked. The rails to Chehaw had been torn up to make bullets. Land holdings had in some cases slipped out of the control of former owners. Now the community was getting its feet on the ground again. Former slaves were adjusting to freedom. They were begging for education, and George W. Campbell was convinced that this was the way to progress. This was a new day, and he wanted young Booker T. Washington to know that there was nothing phony about his interest in educational opportunities for Negroes.

Taking his new acquaintances at their word, Booker began to move swiftly. That is, as swiftly as he could move, using a borrowed cart and a stiff-legged mule for transportation. He had been hired to conduct a school, and he was determined to carry out his assignment. But where, how, and when were the questions he would have to answer—and answer soon. Of one thing he was already certain. The way to build anything, a school, a life, or a civilization, was from the bottom up.

3.

Booker examined or inquired about every building in the town before concluding that the most suitable of those available was a shack next to Butler Chapel, the African Methodist Episcopal Church on Zion Hill. To call one of these structures a shack and the other a church was a technical distinction. They were equally run-down. Neither seemed strong enough to withstand a good wind, but the main advantage of the shack as a school building was its proximity to the church. The larger structure could be used as a sort of assembly hall. The fact that Lewis Adams was the Sunday-school superintendent was also an advantage, as Booker found when he requested the use of these premises.

A location secured, Booker announced, perhaps impetuously, that school would open in a week. He then began to worry about students. Since it had been predetermined that it would be a school for the training of teachers, he decided to have a preliminary look at the country schools in which the teachers would eventually hold classes. Perhaps it would help to learn something about the people whose children they would instruct. At the same time he might announce the opening of his normal school and start enrolling students. Within a few days he began his rounds, using the mule and cart when both were available, just the mule when the cart was in use, and almost immediately a strange new world began to unfold.

It was a world of rolling countryside interspersed with wooded swamps. The places where the inhabitants clustered together in hamlets or on plantations were connected by dusty wagon paths or red dust roads. Booker was drawn to the shoddy cabins in which they lived as by a magnet, and the natural-born sociologist within him began assembling data feverishly.

He met the country folk at their work and asked to be shown their crops. He questioned them about their methods of cultivation, walking back from the fields. At mealtime he accepted their hospitality, and at night he slept in the beds they offered. The fact that the food was limited to salt pork and corn bread did not bother him so much as the observation that the cotton rows outside extended to the very door of the cabin. No space whatever had been set aside for kitchen gardens. Instead, his hosts lived on fat meat and meal purchased from a store in town, at an outlandish price.

Nor was Booker overly embarrassed to find whole families sleeping in a single room. When it became necessary for him to step outside while a wife or daughter prepared for bed, he showed no awkwardness or surprise, for he had himself been born a plantation slave. He was surprised, but not startled, when he came upon fourteen-year-old boys crossing the fields buck naked and their sisters wearing only a single filthy garment, often in rags. So long as there was a pump in the yard with a tub or pan for his own nighttime ablutions, he could stand it. But the discovery of expensive new gadgets of one kind or another in these distressing quarters gave him an unpleasant jolt and sometimes he could not refrain from asking impolite questions.

He learned, in response, that some of the families he visited had paid as much as sixty dollars for sewing machines, generally on installment, and that many of them had purchased elegant clocks costing as much as twelve or fourteen dollars. The crowning example was in a home where Booker was invited to dinner. As he sat down, he noticed that the fork at his place was the only one on the table, though the household consisted of five persons. Booker paused awkwardly, touched and embarrassed by this unusual expression of hospitality. Then it was that his eyes fell upon an organ in the corner. A brand new organ in a home that had only one table fork! Surely, he thought, this indicated the point at which education should begin.

But he had not come into their homes to gape at their ignorance or to deride their foolish aspirations. He had come to make their acquaintance, to recruit students, and to find out what his own job was. Having seen how the folk slept and what food they ate, he shifted his attention to other patterns of family living. He observed that when the day began, "the wife would put a piece of meat in a frying-pan and put a lump of dough in a 'skillet.'" Ten or fifteen minutes later breakfast was ready. As likely as not, the husband would take his portion of bread and meat in his hand and start to the field, munching as he walked. The children would get theirs and scat like young animals, eating as they played, while the mother would take the skillet with whatever remained in it to a corner and make a meal for herself in that way. When meat was scarce, which was often, those who worked in the field were fed first, and the children were deprived.

After breakfast the house was deserted. All who were large enough to carry a hoe worked in the cotton field. The youngest baby was laid down at one end of the patch so that the mother could give it some attention each time she finished chopping a row. The noon and evening meals repeated the pattern of breakfast, and the days from Monday to Friday followed the same routine.

Saturday was different, of course. Saturday was the shopping day. By long-established tradition the whole family spent a good portion, if not all, of that day in town. If one member treasured an old parasol, if another owned a pair of shoes or a dowdy feathered hat, this was the proper occasion. Booker was amused but he was not pleased. He failed to see the point of observing a shopping day without money to spend. He calculated that in most cases "all the shopping that the whole family had money for could have been attended to in ten minutes by one person." Saturdays, he felt, were being misused by these folk worse than the other days.

Rustic churches, big open-air meetings, baptisms in creeks, foot washings, feasts in the wilderness, and other ceremonies of worship drew them on Sunday. Moaning ministers, eyes closed, hands raised, fingers apart, kept them on the edges of their rough benches or brought them to their feet shouting and telling the world how good they felt inside. Booker considered himself a Baptist, he supposed. At least he had attended the Baptist Church in Malden, and he had nothing against organized religion, but he had no taste whatever for this sort of thing, and his manner must have betrayed it. He began to be irritated by the rural preachers. Soon he detected the same kind of feeling on their part toward him.

Booker had ventured into the country as an investigator. Having met the folk in their homes and churches, he turned his attention to the educational facilities. The state, he found, had built no schoolhouses in the districts around Tuskegee. He assumed that it had lacked money for this purpose—an assumption at which many other intelligent young Negroes would have scoffed. They would have asserted that the state simply was unwilling to build schools for rural Negroes. But Booker knew about attitudes too; yet he preferred to keep his mind on the state's obvious impoverishment. When he inquired into the ability of the Negroes to help themselves in this matter, he found that nearly every crop in the counties where he went was mortgaged. The farmers were in debt, pitifully and hopelessly in debt.

They could still dream, of course, and part of their composite dream was reflected in the places they had designated for holding school. Abandoned log cabins and rough-hewn churches were put at the disposal of the teachers in most instances. Often no provision had been made for heating these buildings. The school sessions were casual, to say the least. Sometimes one ran three months, sometimes four, occasionally five, and the apparatus was as limited as these schedules would suggest. A handmade blackboard was a rare luxury. In one of the log cabins visited by Booker he surprised five pupils at study. Two of them sitting together held a book between them. Two others stood behind and read over their shoulders. Behind these two and peeping over their shoulders stood a fifth youngster, also following the reading lesson from the single book.

But Booker had experienced so many hardships he thought little of them one way or the other. The thing that jolted him, as he checked on these schools, was the teachers. That most of them were ignorant was to be expected, perhaps. That many of them were morally deficient was shocking, and Booker had begun to hang his head despondently when he met a fine old Virginian of sixty who snatched him out of his gloomy meditations.

Apparently the fellow was itching to chat, so Booker asked who he was and how he came to be living here. As one Virginian to another, the man smiled warmly and confided that he had been brought to Alabama in 1845.

Sold down the river?

That was it.

How many had been sold at the same time, Booker wanted to know.

"There was five of us," the fellow recalled, "myself and brother and three mules."

Booker rode away feeling better. He did not smile, but inwardly he was laughing—laughing to keep from crying.

4.

When he returned to his lodging in Tuskegee, Booker's mind was popping with ideas, and he was so full of energy, he could scarcely sleep. The next morning was Sunday. Arrangements had been made for him to speak in each of the two colored churches, and Booker found it possible to be at one before the regular preaching began and at the other when it ended. At each he told his story briefly but earnestly and ended by inviting prospective students to call on him at the home of Lewis Adams, where he was rooming, and sign up.

He had scarely finished his breakfast next morning when they began knocking. Some were so young they were accompained by their parents. Many were old enough to be the parents of grown children. Booker had been employed to conduct a normal school for the training of teachers. Well, perhaps that could be loosely interpreted. Even so, he felt compelled to reject those under fifteen years of age and those without any previous education whatever.

When it came to classifying them, his heart sank. A few of the applicants wanted it clearly understood that they would be given advanced standing. They had studied Latin, Greek,

"banking and discount," and a few other equally high-sound-
ing subjects, or so they professed, and naturally they did not
want to be underated. One or two were visibly irked when
Booker casually brushed these empty pretensions aside.
Others stiffened and bided their time. An undercurrent of
resentment began to form. By the end of the week, it had
slowed down student enrollment to such an extent that
Booker found it advisible to go out on the road to see what
he could do.

Near Wilborn's store he met a dusty stranger who looked
tired. The young man examined Booker critically. Could this
be the new professor? He had expected that a professor
would at least be wearing a long-tailed coat on a Sunday
afternoon. Booker was plainly dressed. He had no airs. It
was terribly disappointing.

"You want to go to school here?" Booker asked. Having
left home before daylight that morning, and having walked
all day in the hot sun, William Gregory felt that he had little
choice at this hour of the afternoon. He nodded, and Booker
took out a notebook and enrolled him on the spot.

The next morning, the Fourth of July, 1881, Booker's first
class was called to order in Tuskegee. According to Gregory,
"Everybody was disappointed in Mr. Washington. All of us
could write and make beautiful letters on the board, better
than Mr. Washington, so we did not think he was the right
kind of professor. He examined us and gave each of us a
card telling what classes we were in. I was not up with those
big fellows. They did not notice me, because I was not up
with the others. . . .

"About the second morning he also had us lined up, girls
and boys separately. He examined our cuffs, collars, etc.
Then only one or two fellows had cuffs. Why, he looked us

all over. My clothes were nothing but grease. Mr. Washington said he could not stand those grease spots. Several of us were found dirty and half dressed. Although we thought we were well dressed, Mr. Washington found all these defects in pants, shoes, and everything we had on. The next day everybody had on a collar. They got them downtown, they were cheap just like those paper collars and cuffs, and everybody had their shoes blacked, even old brogans, and everybody stood straight, looking ahead. Mr. Washington kept up that every day and everybody got straight. . . .

"The next morning he began to question everybody right after prayers about what was going on in the country. We did not know. Then there was a newspaper called *The Tuskegee News*. Newspapers were not common, and very few people had a chance to see one. We never read anything but the account of a big fight or something exciting that did not amount to anything; but Mr. Washington wanted to know what was going on around here in the town, in the legislature, and so on, but to us a big shooting or fight was the biggest thing we had. Mr. Washington stopped us from reading that stuff and said to us that that was no news. Everybody was called upon by card to give some item of news. If we did not give some items when called upon, we had to stay out of class until we could. We could not even march or go to class unless we had news."

The enrollment on the first day was thirty, but on July 14 Booker wrote a letter to the *Southern Workman*, the school paper of his alma mater at Hampton, in which he said, "I opened school last week. At present I have over forty students—anxious and earnest young men and women. I expect quite an increase in September and October. The school is taught, at present, in one of the colored churches, which they kindly let us have for that purpose. This building is not very well suited to school purposes, and we hope to be able to move to a more commodious place in a short time. The place referred to is on a beautiful and conveniently located farm of one hundred acres, which we have contracted to buy for $500. The state pays for tuition. The farm I hope to pay for by my own exertions and the help of others here. As a rule, the colored people in the South are not and will not be able for years to board their children in school at ten or twelve dollars per month, hence my object is, as soon as possible, to get the school on a labor basis, so that earnest students can help themselves and at the same time learn the true dignity of labor. An institution for the education of colored youths can be but a *partial* success without a boarding department. In it they can be taught those correct habits which they fail to get at home. Without this part of the training they go out into the world with untrained intellects and their morals and bodies neglected. After the land is paid for, we hope to get a boarding department on foot as soon as possible."

If he was aware of the mixed feelings of his first Tuskegee students, if he detected latent hostility in certain ministers, the young man from Hampton considered neither worth mentioning. "The good-will manifested towards the school by both white and colored is a great encouragment to me to push the work forward. I have had many kind words of encouragement from the whites, and have been well treated by them in every way. The trustees seem to be exceptional men. Whether I have met the colored people in their churches, societies, or homes, I have received their hearty co-operation and a 'God bless you.' Even the colored preachers seem to be highly in favor of the work, and one of the pastors here, fifty years old, is one of my students. I fear I am making my letter too long, I will write again soon."

Taking his courage in his hands, Booker also wrote and dispatched another letter during the tremulous uncertainty of his first month in Alabama, his second week as principal and one-man faculty of the new State Normal School. Though composed with utmost care, this one was not intended for publication. It was addressed with fear and misgiving to J. F. B. Marshall, Treasurer of Hampton Institute, and it contained a request for a loan. Would Hampton, Booker pleaded, let him have two hundred fifty dollars to secure the farm site he had described?

The answer came back as fast as the mails would bring it. The funds of the Institute could not be used to make loans of that kind, not even to its favorite son. However, as an individual, J. F. B. Marshall would be happy to make a personal loan of two hundred dollars—from his own pocket— toward the amount needed.

Booker was not in the habit of kicking up his heels, but neither could he sit still after receiving the money. Within the next four weeks he made a down payment on the Bowen farm, made more mule-back excursions into the rural districts, attended country school-closing exercises conducted by some of his own teacher-students, increased the enrollment of his classes to sixty, began soliciting small donations from local Negroes toward the purchase of the Bowen farm, and wrote hurry-up letters to a talented and attractive young woman teacher recently graduated from the Massachusetts State Normal School at Framingham.

V

LIFE WORK

Booker had to consider ways of angling his appeals for money. "I was about to say," he wrote in his second letter to the *Southern Workman*, that every dollar that we can get out of the colored people themselves, for educational purposes, is worth two coming from elsewhere." In any case, he was thankful to the summer students at Hampton for the way they responded to his first letter. Less than thirty days had elapsed, but with the money they had raised through an entertainment and with what he had been able to solicit locally, he was almost ready to repay the two hundred dollars borrowed from General Marshall. "That the colored people begin to help each other, is the best evidence of their progress. . . . There is hope for an individual or a race when they begin to look outside of themselves."

At twenty-five Booker T. Washington had pretty well formulated the strategy which was to make his public career a phenomenon of American life in decades to follow:

The people of this state have suffered not so much from the failure of the state to support the free schools, but from incompetent teachers. We hope within a few months to make our hum-

ble efforts here felt in the surrounding counties. Of course we
have to labor under many disadvantages, not having apparatus,
school furniture and suitable buildings. This ought not to be so,
for when teachers come here thirsty for knowledge and with only
money enough to remain in school a few months, we ought to be
able to give them the best advantages at once. Some of these wants
are being supplied by friends and we hope in a few months to
double the advantages of the school. There is much that is encouraging in the work. The students are anxious to improve and
they pin themselves down to study without coercion.

The editor, General Armstrong himself, called the effort
"most praiseworthy." Commenting on the contributions already sent by friends and former associates at Hampton, he
offered to forward help from any others to the "Tuskegee
Normal School for the Education of Colored Teachers, B.
T. Washington, Principal."

Readers of the *Workman,* past and present students of
Hampton, teachers and friends of the Institute would have
been keenly interested in another bit of news as well. But
Booker refrained from mentioning the new teacher who had
just arrived to assist him, even though she too was a Hampton graduate, class of '79, and had been recommended for
the post by General Armstrong.

Two years older than Booker, fair enough to pass as white,
Olivia A. Davidson had just completed a two-year course of
studies at the Massachusetts State Normal School at Framingham. But it was while growing up in Ohio, attending the
public schools of that state, to which her family had moved
from Virginia, that she had first felt her sympathies drawn
to the new freedmen. Thereafter she had wasted no time.
Still in her teens, she had offered herself as a teacher in
Mississippi, along with her older brother.

But the work of young teachers in that state, the two had discovered, could not be limited to instruction in the three R's. When one of Olivia's pupils came down with smallpox, terror gripped the community. Neighbors, friends, and even relatives fled from the house where the sick boy lay on his pallet, but the girl from Ohio refused to leave the bedside of the stricken child.

The real ordeal came later. The Ku Klux Klan objected to the activties of missionary teachers among the freedmen, whether by Northern whites from New England or near-whites from Ohio like Olivia and her brother. They warned and threatened, as was their custom. When the boy and his sister went right on teaching, the mob returned by night, dragged the boy out, and lynched him. That ended Olivia's stay in Mississippi, but she did not go home. Instead, she accepted a school in Memphis.

She had not been in the new situation long when the worst yellow-fever epidemic on record broke out. She was back in Ohio on a short but badly needed vacation when the schools were officially closed, but she promptly wired the mayor volunteering to serve as a nurse. Since she had never had yellow fever, however, her offer was declined. Haunted by these memories, her faith in God admittedly shaken, she had set her mind on Hampton, where she enrolled in 1878 and graduated with honors the very next year. While there, she had been introduced by one of her young instructors to his aunt, Mrs. Mary Hemenway, a lady of Boston who had come to visit the school.

In May of 1870, just five months after the first public meeting in Boston on behalf of General Armstrong's work, Mrs. Hemenway had contributed five hundred dollars toward the building fund. In December of the same year she had given another five hundred dollars, and this was just a beginning. She contributed $3,488.31 to the same fund in March of the following year. In June of 1873, when Booker was completing his first year at the Institute, she was thanked publicly for "a complete set of brass band instruments." By the time Olivia Davidson came to Hampton as a student, Mrs. Hemenway and various other Hemenways, apparently related, were listed among the contributors of annual tuition scholarships.

Herbert A. Chenoweth represented another facet of her interest. A young white man of Lynn, he was working as a clerk in the Boston Post Office when Mrs. Hemenway discovered him. She was intrigued by his interest in a cooperative bank. He had acquired forty-five shares as well as other business holdings, and now his idea was to start cooperative banks in the South. Such an enterprise, he was convinced, would "enable the colored people to build their own homes very easily." Mrs. Hemenway "educated" him and bundled him off to Hampton, where he arrived in time to become a member of Olivia Davidson's class.

But Olivia became Mrs. Hemenway's special protege, and when she graduated from Hampton in 1879 Mrs. Hemenway promptly arranged for her training at Framingham. The fact that Booker and Olivia had met at Hampton, that she had heard him give his most successful speech to date, may or may not have simplified correspondence. But within six weeks after he opened the school at Tuskegee, she was by his side.

Book learning, they promptly decided, putting their heads together, would never be enough for their pupils. The miserable homes from which they came or in which they boarded while at Tuskegee nullified everything Miss Davidson or Mr.

Washington could teach in their classes about personal cleanliness, good eating habits, industry, care of rooms, and thrift.
Both of them dreamed, as General Armstrong had advocated,
of teaching young Negroes useful skills which would enable
them to earn money as freedmen, buy homes, start businesses, climb the economic ladder. But how to start, that
was the question.

Well, their first observation was that most of their students
came from farms and that they would return to their own
communities to teach other young people who lived on farms.
About 85 percent of all Southern Negroes lived in the country. To Booker and Oivia that said just one thing. Their first
concern should be to avoid educating their pupils "out of
sympathy with agricultural life."

As old plantations go, the Bowen estate, about a mile out
of town, wasn't much. The big house had been burned during the War. Abandoned since emancipation, the property
had gone to weeds. But Booker Washington and Olivia
Davidson decided that everything about it was right for their
school.

2.

Booker could not hide his elation as he broke the news of
their move to the would-be teachers in his classes, but the
calmness with which they received the announcement
sobered him. They were familiar with the abandoned Bowen
place: the two cabins, one of which had served the former
plantation owners as a kitchen and the other as a dining
room, the old stable, the chicken house. Yes, they knew. And
as a place for a school they did not consider it much of an
improvement on their present quarters.

Booker admitted that the property was run down. What he had in mind, of course, was renovation, rebuilding. The grounds were ample. They could be cleared and tilled again. The cabins, the stable—yes, even the chicken house could be cleaned and adapted to some educational use.

His students began to mutter. Chopping through thickets, cleaning up old stables and chicken houses—that was work, hard, dirty work. Did Mr. Washington know what he was saying? Did he have someone in mind for all that labor?

He nodded. Yes, he did. He was thinking about *them.* They all looked strong and capable to him. He assumed they had worked with their hands back on the plantations where they lived. His idea was to have them put the Bowen place in shape and eventually to build their own school. He put it to them bluntly and then watched as their expressions changed from puzzlement to disappointment and finally resentment.

But they were students, they blurted. They were not laborers or fields hands. Many of them had already taught school. Had he forgotten? Now it was Booker's turn to look pained.

When he broached the subject again, he had his coat off. He was wearing his roughest clothes and carrying a borrowed ax. He was on his way to the school property, he told them. He was inviting the male students to equip themselves in the same way and come along.

They followed reluctantly. As soon as they got up a good sweat, their reluctance vanished, however. It was not that they disliked work, Booker mused, but that they had the wrong idea about it. His job was to convince them that work was dignified and honorable. They had never seen refined people digging and scrubbing. The people of quality they had observed on Southern plantations never dirtied their hands. Hard, back-bending work was for low-down folks.

While they had been disappointed at first in the simplicity of their young professor, they had never been foolish enough to think him low-down or common. If Booker Washington could dig stumps, clear away brush, whitewash walls of cabins, so could they. If Miss Davidson, tidy and refined, could go from door to door in the town soliciting chickens and cakes, ham and pies for a Saturday night supper to raise money to help pay the borrowed money, so could the young women students. Thereafter work on the new premises became part of the school day. When classes were dismissed, everyone put on working clothes and headed for the farm on the outskirts of Tuskegee.

Before long they were so pleased with the results they could not be stopped. Not only were chicken house, stable, and cabins transformed by broom and whitewash bucket into classrooms, but the grounds around them were chopped and raked and swept till no one could be ashamed of them. During those early weeks another young Hampton graduate, John R. Cardwell, arrived to assist with the teaching, especially the music, and the Tuskegee Normal School for the Education of Colored Teachers was no longer limited to the the shanty next to the African Methodist Episcopal Zion Church.

A few weeks later, golden autumn leaves still clinging to the trees outside, Booker fell into a reflective mood and sat down to take stock, addressing his words to the *Southern Workman:*

Four months and a half ago, without a dollar of our own, we contracted to buy a farm of one hundred acres, at a cost of $500, on which to permanently locate our school. Today the last dollar has been paid. While most of the money to pay for the farm has come from the North, the people here have not failed to help themselves. Almost one month ago, when we wanted but one hundred dollars more to complete the payment on the land, we resolved to raise that amount here in Alabama. To do this, three plans were put on foot. First, the students were to give a literary entertainment; second, a supper of festival was to come the next week after the entertainment; third, two of the leading citizens were appointed to solicit subscriptions among the whites and colored.

The students were made to understand that others were willing to help them provided they did something for themselves. With this in view they went to work, taking as little time for preparations from their regular studies as possible. In a few weeks all had their parts well learned. On the night of the exhibition, each student seemed to feel a personal responsibility. There was an air of earnestness and order in everything they did. The entertainment was attended by a good house of colored citizens and some whites. One of the latter, who had already subscribed five dollars towards paying for the land, was so well pleased with the entertainment that he sent up word at the close that he would give five dollars more. Another one said that it was the best exhibition of its kind he had ever attended. From this entertainment we netted over $20.00. Directly afterwards we began preparations for the supper, Miss Davidson taking the lead. That we might incur as little expense as possible, each student having parents or friends living in town was asked to get them to give something towards the supper. Five ladies here in town kindly volunteered to assist Miss Davidson in carrying out the supper. An hour was appointed for contributions to be brought to the hall. It was a real pleasure and encouragement to see how generously the people responded. A long table was soon laden with cakes, turkeys, chickens &., &. At night the people turned out *en masse*. In this also the students did not fail to do their part. The girls in our junior or highest class, originated the idea of their having a table of fancy candies, &. They begged the money with which to carry out their plan, and from that table we realiezd a handsome sum. Some of the girls attended the table, while others would drum up customers. One girl played the 'peanut woman' well through the crowd, while one little fellow peddled apples for his share of the work, and another one candy. To make sure of a good attendance at the hall, fifteen young men formed themselves into a committee to canvas different parts of the town. From the supper we cleared $50.00.

While we were in the midst of carrying out the above named plans, we were very pleasantly surprised by receiving a donation of $100.00 from a lady in Boston, who has never failed to help the Negro to help himself; and in a few days more a letter came from a generous friend in Connecticut, who had already given us $200.00 towards paying for the land, saying that if we would raise $115.00 (the amount then due on the land,) in Alabama by the first of next January, he would donate to us $100.00 more with which to buy tools, seeds, &., for the equipment of the farm. We only want twenty-six dollars more to comply with his proposition. We will get it.

Now that the farm is paid for, it should not be permitted to remain idle. Our students are too badly in need of the aid which can come from it. We want to put in a crop as soon as the weather permits. To do this we need stock, vehicles, tools, a stable, cash to pay for first year's labor, &. What a lift it would be to our students could we get the three or four hundred dollars needed to make this start.

One thing that probably retards the progress of education in the Normal and other high schools in the South more than anything else is the 'in and out' system. Few students are able to remain in school an entire term because they are *not able to pay board*. More than once this term, when students have stayed here till their last dollar was spent, have they come to me with tears in their eyes to say, 'I must go.' Several are cooking for themselves, that they may squeeze through the term. We do not want our students to become objects of charity. We only want to make the school able to give them a *chance to help themselves.* Our plan will have two advantages, first, it will permit the students to remain in school, secondly, it will teach them how to labor.

In the South, education of the head and hand must go together. While the girl learns arithmetic she must learn to set a table, or she will never learn it. Trained farmers are as much needed as trained teachers.

As soon as the farm is equipped, we expect to direct our energies towards getting up a school building by next term. The present buildings on the farm will be entirely insufficient to accommodate the school next term. We may seem to be planning much, but remembering that God helps those who help themselves, we will go forward.

Yours faithfully,
B. T. Washington

3.

Was he getting ahead of himself? Had he said too much in one letter? His friends at Hampton would understand, General Armstrong included, but how about the three thousand readers of the *Southern Workman*? Booker knew that these represented a cross section of Northern philanthropy and included key figures among the more aspiring members of his own race, as well as a roll call of Hampton graduates. Would these readers suspect him of trying to run before he could walk?

Fortunately, he had in his possession another letter, one he had received in response to the two letters he had previously written for publication. Perhaps this would ease possible misgivings.

General Armstrong was in full accord. Publishing the note in the same issue, he added a few comments of his own: "A gentleman who for over fifty years has been an active friend of the colored race, accompanied a recent generous gift to our graduate, Mr. B. T. Washington's effort in the Tuskegee Normal School, with a letter so full of kindly and valuable counsel that we fully agree with Mr. Washington's wish to give it a wider audience; only regretting that we may not add to it the force of the writer's name."

While is is very important to learn to read, write and cipher, it is equally important to learn to work, and to form the habit of industry. At great cost of life and treasure, your race have obtained freedom and the right of suffrage. Now what you need is knowledge and independence, which can only be obtained, each one for him or herself, by hard study and diligent labor. Never spend a penny for anything without full consideration of the necessity of doing it. Industry and economy lead to independence. Wealth does not always secure independence. The man with a saw-buck, who saws wood for a living, who owes no man anything, except love and good well, who lives and provides for those dependent on him with his daily earnings, is often more independent than many men with more money.

Self reliance and self respect are important for every man and woman to have,—not pride, but consciousness of the will and ability to make a place for themselves in the world. Spend no time making a reputation; they are often made and destroyed in an hour; but look well to the character you are making;—this the work of a lifetime. A good character for honesty, industry,—for good will to all men, with a will and desire to do right to all; with that love to God and man, which is our reasonable service; forms a character like the marble column;—pure and white, and is only stained or marred by our own wrongdoing. The color of a man or woman will not blemish the white column; bad conduct, unkind feelings towards others will, whether they have a black or a white skin.

The true glory of a man or woman is goodness:—not wealth or learning, both of which it is important to have if we make good use of them in doing good to others.

For more than fifty years I have taken a deep interest in your race, and labored for their freedom until it was obtained, and since they have been made free, I have a strong desire that by their sobriety, their industry, their diligence in well-doing, they may prove to the world that they are worthy, and that they will make a good return for all that has been done for them.

With my best wishes for your success in your efforts to raise up teachers, and to do good to your race, and to all men; with kind regard to all your teachers, and scholars, as well as yourself,

I am yours truly.

P.S. I like the pleasure of giving, but not the notoriety; therefore do not wish my name published in connection with anything I do.

Elsewhere in the same issue General Armstrong indulged in a few more words on tht budding career of his favorite student and disciple, under the heading, "A Child of Hampton."

A year ago, the State Superintendent of Public Instruction of Alabama wrote to the Principal of Hampton Institute for a Hampton graduate to establish and superintend a new Normal School for colored teachers, for which the Board had decided to appropriate $2,000 for teachers' salaries. Mr. Booker T. Washington, of the class of '76, then teacher in charge of Indian young men at Hampton, was heartily recommended for the position, with Miss Olivia Davidson, who, after a year at Hampton, graduated in the class of '79, and afterwards at the Framingham, (Mass.) Normal School, for his assistant. On assuming his charge, Mr. Washington soon found the great necessity of providing some means of self-help for his students, and an opportunity presenting itself to secure a small farm on reasonable terms, he ventured to try it, with help of a loan from a friend at Hampton which he has already paid. The rest of the story we leave to him to tell. In this courageous enterprise of two of her graduates for their people, this young offshoot of her own ideas and teachings, Hampton feels a very special interest, and knowing the workers has faith in its success.

"I love my work more and more," Booker responded with feeling." My children seem eager to learn; to ask them not to do a thing is all that is necessary. One who cared to work for others at all, could not be discouraged. We never dream of discouragement; never speak of it; all our dreams, and thoughts, and talk are of success; success is our aim, and it will be our end."

Time had passed so swiftly and so much had happened in his first half year in Alabama, Booker and Olivia had both forgotten about the holiday season. A sharp knock on his door snatched him out if his dream, however. A band of children was standing in the darkness. "Chris'mus gift!" they chorused as he cracked the door a few inches. "Chris'mus gift, professor!"

They had him. Standing with a kerosene lamp in his hand, blinking nearsightedly and shivering a little in the cool air, he could only nod assent and stumble back into the kitchen to forage in the crocks and tins for a cooky, an apple, a handful of pecans, something he could offer the ragged youngsters of the town.

When they were gone, he noticed that it was scarcely two

o'clock. He slept little thereafter, partly because he was intrigued by the survival of the slavery-time custom of begging for gifts on Christmas morning, partly because the first group was followed by a succession of others, repeating the same demands till daybreak. A few hours later he got an idea of what he could expect during the rest of the week.

If he had any serious plans for those days, he might as well put them on the shelf, he was told. Another slavery-time custom that nobody around Tuskegee had suggested abolishing was the full week of Christmas celebration. Not many folks would be sober enough to listen to anything the professor had to say during that period. Even those who ordinarily drank no whiskey or gin seemed to feel that it was the only proper thing to do, come Christmas. Naturally all who had guns or pistols brought them out and fired them into the night air. Any harsh noise or explosion, they seemed to feel, was an added note of festivity.

Booker was horrified, but not because he had never seen such carrying on before. The miners around Malden could give a noisy account of themselves when they felt like it. He had witnessed more than one kind of high jinks in Washington, D. C., and elsewhere, but somehow he had let himself believe that the colored folks of Tuskegee were different. He had boasted of their wholesomeness as compared to their city cousins. And now this! He decided to get as far away from it as possible. Borrowing the old mule that had been put at his disposal in the past, he headed for the country.

What he saw, unfortunately, was not much help to his frame of mind. Abject poverty seemed to be acentuated by the pathetic attempts of the country people to catch a little of the Christmas spirit. Booker looked into one cabin in which a parent was dividing a single bunch of firecrackers among five children. In another he saw ten cents' worth of stale ginger cake split six ways in memory of Christ's birthday. Another family had spent their Christmas money for a few stalks of sugar cane. A rustic preacher and his wife, Booker found, were celebrating with a jug of cheap whiskey. Another was prepared to convince Booker that God had cursed all labor because of Adam and Eve's conduct in the Garden of Eden. Christmas week, therefore, was the only week of this individual's year that was entirely free from sin.

If Booker had needed a reminder that his work in Alabama had scarcely begun, despite the kind words of those who sought to encourage him, this was it. When school opened again after the vacation, he let his students know how he felt. Not only was there no time for nonsense when classes were called, but after school and on weekends he kept them reminded. Only limited progress could be made while they continued to live in homes which so quickly and completely neutralized the influences of his school. To succeed at all, he and his teachers would need full-time supervision over the students. A boarding department was absolutely basic.

Pausing only long enough to deed the newly acquired farm to a board of nine trustees, composed of Northern as well as Southern members, Booker and Olivia launched a drive for a school building. None of the momentum from the earlier campaign was lost. But whereas the neglected Bowen plantation on the outskirts of Tuskegee had cost five hundred dollars, their first estimate of the cost of the school building they wanted was nearly ten times that figure.

However, they were less dismayed by this prospect than Booker had been when he undertook the first drive. Not only were there two of them to consult together in making the decision, but they had in common a certain amount of useful experience in raising money for an educational purpose. They had the goodwill and support of the families and friends of young people who had attended their classes. They had the encouragement of white people as well as colored in Tuskegee. These factors could be counted as more than intangibles. But more important still, they had Hampton's warmest blessing, and with this anything was possible.

Early in 1882 Booker and Olivia decided to make the cornerstone laying for the new building the main feature of their first school-closing exercises.

4.

March 30, 1882, was the date. The young people brought armfuls of roses the evening before, and with these the church was decorated and perfumed. Above the temporary platform, with its chairs facing the audience, an arch of roses was constructed. Bouquets and wreaths were placed in every space that would accommodate them.

Soon after dawn the folk from the country began arriving. They intended to see everything. The exercises began at ten with class recitations before the visitors. At eleven thirty a procession formed on the grounds around the church and marched out to the farm. En route it was joined by the carriages of the mayor, several pastors of local churches, a number of businessmen and other townsfolk.

After a brief cornerstone ceremony, Waddy Thompson, county superintendent of education, mounted the platform, acknowledged a generous introduction, and began speaking. The sun was hot, and there was no shade near the spot where the stone had been placed, but the listeners remained attentive with heads bare, many of them inwardly braced for the kind of thing they were frequently obliged to listen to from prominently placed men of the Old South.

"The State Superintendent of Education, Honorable H. Clay Armstrong, expected to be present here today, and perform the work which I have attempted; but I received a note from him a few days ago requesting me to represent him on this occasion as he thought it important that he should attend a meeting of State Superintendents which convened at Washington about this time," Waddy Thompson began, unmpromisingly. He improved as he went along, however, and soon he was saying such things as, "No state is great until its educational facilities are great, and placed at the door of the poor boy in the cabin, as well as in the reach of the child of wealth and fortune. . . . When you scatter the darkness of the mind by the light of knowledge, you make better citizens, better workmen in shops, better farmers in the field, better merchants, and mechanics, and associates cooperating in all the circles of business. . . . This is perhaps an occasion of greater interest to the colored people than the rest of us, because it marks the beginning of a new era in their history. We have today for the first time witnessed the laying of the foundation of a building to be erected and used solely for their education. Perhaps there are some here today whose minds are shrouded by the night of ignorance, and they cannot now fully understand or appreciate the importance of this event, but in years to come, they will look back to this time as eventful in their history. . . ."

Booker was frankly surprised to hear this kind of talk from a Southerner such as Waddy Thompson. He and Olivia took most of the speech down in writing. If this was the mind of

the educated South, or a representative part of it, he felt
that friends of the Negro should become aware of the area
of common ground which it suggested. Indeed, here were
some ideas and insights which could be used in many ways.
He would have to come back to them again when there was
more time. Today there were other events on the program.

Dinner followed the speaking. Some magnificent old trees,
cedars, mulberries, and magnolias, reminders of the halycon
days of Colonel Bowen's plantation, were still standing, still
beautifully suited to picnic baskets. At two o'clock the procession formed again and returned to the church for a rhetor-
ical program consisting of essays, recitations, and songs by
the students themselves. Young men and women who would
soon be teaching in one-room schools of the state read carefully written and rehearsed compositions on "Habits," "The
Teacher's Work," "Home," "The Colored Citizens of Alabama," and "Normal Schools." Others, whose home addresses
were given as Opelika, Cotton Valley, Gueryton, and Fort
Mitchell as well as Tuskegee, recited "The Charcoal Man,"
"The Drunkard's Daughter," "Curfew Must not Ring Tonight," and "Waiting."

At the conclusion of these exercises the pastor of the
largest colored church in Montgomery was called upon. He
spoke with deep feeling, indicating that he too had been
struck by the significance of Waddy Thompson's remarks.
"I have witnessed today something I never saw before, nor
nor did I expect to see it," Reverend C. C. Petty observed. "I
have seen one who but yesterday was one of our owners
today lay the cornerstone of a building devoted to the education of my race. For such a change let us all thank God."

The pastor of one of the white churches of Tuskegee came
next. Then Booker spoke. He wanted only to thank the local

people for their interest and help in the work he and the other teachers were trying to do. But evidently he said it just right. After the benediction there was much crowding toward the front. Everybody seemed eager to shake his hand and the hand of Olivia. Most of them wanted to say "God bless you" or words to that effect before leaving. They were determined that Booker should know that his first year's work had the stamp of their approval.

He couldn't have asked for more. In fact, he felt inspired. The enromous challenge of the months ahead, in which he and Olivia had virtually committed themselves to raise nearly four thousand dollars, in addition to a thousand already collected in small donations, to erect the school building whose cornerstone had just been laid on sheer faith, seemed as nothing. Together they could do it. With Olivia to assist, almost anything seemed possible. They had talked it over. The plans had been made.

But one thing at a time. The first step in the campaign was to prepare and publish a pamphlet giving an explicit account of their work to date and itemizing all monies received and spent and making a statement of future plans and needs. That done, the two of them would be ready to head for the North, resuming the talks before churches, clubs, and any other sympathetic groups that would hear them, as well as the door-to-door personal solicitations, the never dull but never easy routine of fund raising at which they had both gained experience and learned some techniques during the past year.

On his way North, of course, Booker had another errand. Fanny Smith, whom he had known since childhood in Malden and courted since she was old enough to court, was now herself graduating from Hampton with the class of '82. She was twenty-four years old, a brown-skinned girl whom no one, not even Booker or her teachers at Hampton, ever bothered actually to describe. Indeed, the thing about her that impressed him most, aside from the fact that she was his first love, was "her extreme neatness in her housekeeping and general work. Nothing was done loosely or carelessly." The time had come for him to marry Fanny Smith.

When he returned to Tuskegee in August, Fanny was with him, and they set up their home in one of the cottages on the farm. Arrangements were made for the four other teachers, including a young high-school graduate from Washington, D.C., named R. S. Pannott, whose experience in the public schools of that city had been in the teaching of vocal music, Margaret E. Snodgrass, and Lucy E. Smith, both Hampton graduates in Olivia's class and both experienced in elementary teaching, and Olivia herself, to board with them. Fanny's role became that of housekeeper.

But Olivia was still up North raising money, and the new school building was going up faster than the donations were coming in. Creditors began to hound Booker as he pressed the workmen to get the structure up in time for the opening of school, on the one hand, and tried to hold at bay those on whom they depended for materials, on the other. For several weeks he scarcely slept, and there were nights when the specter of failure haunted him. Some of the costs were running higher than he had calculated. Now that he was back at Tuskegee, it began to seem that Olivia's solicitations were slowing down. Had she worked too hard? Her letters indicated how tired she was. What if Olivia should break down? Certainly all would be lost. Even now the situation was critical. One of the local creditors was getting ugly about a bill for four hundred dollars. He would be out for a showdown next day.

The mail came before he arrived, however, and in it a letter from Olivia enclosing her solicitations to date—exactly four hundred dollars. Booker braced himself again, counting heavily on the admittedly frail physical resources of his assistant in the field. He dug in where the builders were at work. He wrote letters. A substantial gift from Mr. A. H. Porter came at a crucial moment, and by the first of September it was assured that the building could be finished, though not in time for the announced opening of school on the fourth. It would be necessary to request the continued use of the old shanties and the church again, pending a few more weeks of work on the building, which he now proposed to call Porter Hall.

Olivia returned, and there was a breathing spell in which the matter of funds was not desperate, but another problem suddenly became urgent. Prior to the fall of 1882 no Methodist child in Tuskegee had ever attended school with a Baptist child, so far as Booker could determine. As a result, public schools were not only segregated racially but denominationally. This meant that two schools had to be maintained for Negro children. Neither of them amounted to much, but they were necessary to the practice teaching of Booker's normal students. Securing the use of them for this purpose meant taking over the whole responsibility for their teaching and administration. Under these conditions the question of the separate Methodist and Baptist elementary schools posed a problem.

It was a problem of tact and diplomacy, but Booker and Olivia took it on without hesitation. First the consent of the folk living and working on the farm had to be secured. When these were brought around, the work with the interested parties in the town began. Eventually an agreement to combine the schools and let Booker and Olivia operate them on their new premises as a training school for their normal students was obtained.

So it was again possible to think in terms of enrolling students and conducting classes. On September 4 the second school year began with somewhat more than twice the number of students enrolled during the first two months of the first year. Morale was high, thanks in part to the return of a certain number of "old" students, some of whom had spent the summer teaching in the outlying counties. They had experiences to tell. All began at once to look forward with their teachers to the day when they could quit their shabby temporary quarters and move into the new schoolhouse on the old Bowen plantation.

The second date set for moving was November 1. When this could not be met, Thanksgiving was named as the time, and this was achieved. In fact, they were able to hold Thanksgiving Day exercises in the chapel, which occupied most of the second floor of the new building. More than a hundred students had been enrolled by then, and these occupied only about a third of the total seating space in the auditorium, but no one suggested for a moment that the new place was too large. Had they called in the children from the elementary school, they could have actually filled it immediately, as they did that evening and again the following evening with visitors from the community. On these two nights and the Saturday which followed Olivia held a fair to raise money for the school. The other teachers helped, and the results were gratifying, especially on Friday night, the occasion of the "jug breaking." A month earlier twelve competing students had been provided with jugs into which small coins could be dropped. When these were broken open before the crowd, there was much excitement. The forty-five dollars that the jugs yielded made huge piles of nickels and pennies. Other income from the fair amounted to an additional one hundred dollars.

Booker thanked all who had helped. Then he reminded the students that while they rejoiced and gave thanks, there remained much work to be done. True, they had a nice chapel room now, the adjoining room could serve as a library; above them on the third floor was dormitory space with rooms to accommodate fifty young women students, and on the floor below there were recitation rooms and a room for the principal's office, but all could see that the basement had scarcely been touched. A large amount of earth would have to be removed before the work could be done which would transform it into a dining hall.

Before he could finish talking, a young man wanted to say something. Since kind friends, North and South, near and far, had contributed nearly all the money required to erect this building for their benefit, he thought he and the other men students ought to do something more toward it. If they were to pitch in and dig out all that dirt in the basement, that alone, as he calculated, would be worth about thirty or thirty-five dollars. Another youth backed him up, adding the suggestion that they divide themselves into squads, that the squads take turns working an hour a day after school. Approval was general, and on this note the Thanksgiving celebration ended.

A week later Booker wrote to General Armstrong. Thanking him for still another substantial gift from one of those anonymous sources which seemed so numerous in those days, he ventured to add, "I hope you will not think me assuming too much. We want very much to have a Christmas tree or something of the kind for our students. . . . they know so little of such luxuries. I write to ask if you could, with propriety, suggest the matter to some friend [up] North. We could provide something ourselves, but the efforts we have had to make for our building leave us with but few resources."

5.

The tree was provided, of course, and there was genuine holiday cheer at Christmas time, but the pattern of hinderances and furtherances in the progress of the young school was not altered as the year 1883 began. Booker was not one to publicize his drawbacks, but that did not entirely dispose of them. In some cases they had to do with matters entirely beyond his control. Booker had dared to hope for a modest increase in the state's annual appropriation for salaries, on the basis of the year's work and the outside assistance he and Olivia had been able to obtain. Without an increase of at least a thousand dollars in the money from the state, it was hard to figure how salaries could be paid to the additional teachers they had employed. Booker was somewhat encouraged by an invitation to make a statement about his work to the committee of the Senate which was concerned with the appropriation, but anxiety increased as the time approached.

He went down to Montgomery on the appointed day and told his story in the committee room, laying special stress on industrial education, as he called it. When he saw that the legislators were interested, he enlarged. Industrial education was the cornerstone of his faith. At Tuskegee he was not only teaching the dignity of labor, he was practicing it. One might say that they were already conducting their first industry in the school. It was farming. Part of the newly acquired farm was being cultivated with student help. The students had done much of the actual construction work in their new building. That was the way he approached the matter. His definition of education was teaching students to do the common work that fell to their hands: agriculture, building, domestic service, whatever was useful, whatever was necessary. That the whole South, and not just the Negro, would benefit by increasing the number of such trained hands, he felt, went without saying.

Whether he knew it or not, he had them in the palm of his hand before he finished. They were sold. Nor would there have been any doubt as to their ability to secure the needed legislation had not complications developed over night. The state treasurer of Alabama was reported absent with something like a quarter of a million dollars of the state's money. What this was likely to do to Booker's plea for an increase in the appropriation to his school was not hard to imagine.

Fearing the worst, Colonel W. F. Foster, now the Speaker of the House, rose dramatically and left his chair to support the request from the floor, when it was introduced. The others who had listened to Booker in the committee lined up behind him, and together they mustered a big majority. The one thousand dollars was added. What was more, H. Clay Armstrong was suddenly heard from. The state superintendent of education who had not been able to serve at the laying of the cornerstone, due to a meeting in Washington, but who insisted his interest in the Tuskegee school was sincere, notified Booker that he had talked to J. T. M. Carey of the Peabody Fund in its behalf. As a result five hundred dollars from that source was now available to Booker's work for operations during the coming year.

In the midst of these windfalls an individual in Connecticut, whose interest they were quietly cultivating, suddenly came through with money for the purchase of an additional forty acres of pasture and woodland adjoining the farm. All told, the outlook was enormously encouraging in late February, when Booker remembered that he owed General Armstrong a letter. How hard he had worked to bring about some of the results that appeared to have been achieved by magic was Booker's own secret. Nor was he disposed to speak of the anxiety he sometimes felt while trying to cope with such a variety of problems. Neither the work nor the worry was enough to upset a young man of Booker's capacity at this stage, but they did keep him reminded that this talk about another Hampton, about building an industrial institute in Alabama like the one General Armstrong had established in Virginia, with dormitories and classroom buildings, workshops and barns, cottages and cultivated fields, towers and trees scattered across the landscape, was going to be more than a notion.

Success would depend in large measure on the kindness of local friends, Booker knew, but here, too, the outlook was good. "It is certainly a cheering sign to see how interested some of the leading Southern whites are becoming in the education of the Negro," he said in his letter, referring to the backing he was getting from Colonel Foster. Men like G. W. Campbell, the president of the Board of Commissioners and William B. Swanson were among the oldest and most respected citizens of Macon County. All were solidly

behind him and the school. The same could be said for the
Reverend R. C. Bedford, pastor of the Congregational Church
in Montgomery. Reverend Bedford had just paid the school
a visit, sat in on classes for two days, inspected the grounds,
and addressed a chapelful of community people in the evening. Back in his pastoral study again, he was so carried
away by his impressions of the twenty-six-year-old Booker
and the work he was doing at Tuskegee that he could not
resist the temptation to write a long letter of commendation
to the young teacher's mentor, General Armstrong. In his
enthusiasm Reverend Bedford was probably unaware of a
few exaggerations, such as saying that the new school building had four stories, when actually it had only three, but he
had checked his own estimate of "Professor Washington and
his associates" with those of key people in that part of the
state and he could testify that their attitude was good.

Meanwhile another friendly visitor headed for Tuskegee.
General J. F. B. Marshall, treasurer of Hampton Institute,
had been ordered to take a few days rest. What could be
more stimulating to an overworked treasurer than a leisurely
journey through the Confederacy he had once helped to
subdue? Certainly nothing that General Marshall could think
of at the moment, unless it was to have a close look at the
progress of a Hampton youth he had backed with his own
money. Here, he thought, was a way to do both at once.

6.

His first layover was in Richmond. General Marshall strolled
down a fashionable street between trains, taking in the sights,
admiring the "seven-hilled city." He reacted sharply to the

symbolism of a poster he saw depicting a "handsomely dressed child, in an agony of grief because he had broken the staff of a pretty American flag which he was carrying over his shoulders . . . being comforted with the promise of a new one." The old warrior turned philanthropist couldn't help recalling a time when "that child's young life would not have been safe under the Stars and Stripes in that city."

Back in the room where he was lodged as a transient, he scanned the pages of a local newspaper. He was astonished when he came across an announcement "that a batallion of State Colored troops would turn out in full uniform on Tuesday, to escort into the city Hon. Frederick Douglass, who was to deliver a lecture." Virginia's state troops, rank and file, ex-slaves, escorting with honor a runaway slave into the late capital of the Confederacy! He could scarcely believe it. Again his mind turned backwards, this time to a scene that had revolted him in his native Massachusetts: the capture and return, despite roars of protest and public indignation, of the fugitive slave Burns. Certainly this was a far cry from that situation.

Obliged to wait over Sunday for a train going south, the touring General elected to worship with the congregation of the well-favored and much-talked-about "Preacher Holmes," a Negro minister who had just succeeded in erecting a rather spectacular new edifice for his more than three thousand members. Pleased when the preacher recognized him as an official of Hampton Institute, General Marshall's heart sank when the notices were read. These included "some dozen of pathetic inquiries from ex-slaves for wives, children, or other relatives who had been sold South." This after the eighteen years that had elapsed since the end of the War was a sobering reminder.

In Atlanta he encountered an "immense concourse of Georgians from all parts of the state, who had assembled to pay the last tribute of respect to their beloved leader, Governor Alexander H. Stephens." Marshall had run into an old friend from Boston, the Reverend George L. Chaney, down there, and they had decided to attend the services. That afternoon they watched the funeral pass. "The procession was nearly two miles in length, and among the handsomely uniformed troops which, with reversed arms, followed to his grave the late vice-president of the Confederacy, whose cornerstone he declared to be slavery, were eleven companies of colored troops of the state, whose bearing and appearance compared very favorably with that of the white troops." The talk was that Stephens, at the time of his death, was personally paying for the education of twenty young men, a large proportion of whom were freedmen. That struck General Marshall as convincing evidence that "the war was over." This was still his mood when he finally got off the train at Chehaw, five miles from Tuskegee.

Booker T. Washington was waiting at the depot beside "a ramshackle buggy which looked as if it would fall to pieces if the coating of red mud were washed off, a dilapidated harness and a nag whose every step was taken under protest, except once when suddenly the screech of the locomotive galvanized him into a short but lively run." General Marshall chuckled. The nag, the conveyance, everything that met his eye was a reminder of "the early days of the Hampton school . . . our beginnings and our methods." He wouldn't have wanted it otherwise.

They reached the farm, and Booker conducted him on an inspection tour. The new building, still not entirely completed, General Marshall noticed, was not unlike Hampton's

Academic Hall. The primary school, taught by two young Hampton women, was the counterpart of their alma mater's Butler School, but here the resemblance ended. Miss Snodgrass and Miss Smith were conducting their classes "in what was an old stable and hen house." Their youngsters were "packed as close as crayons in a Waltham box." He thought it worth mentioning that all six of the teachers were colored. At Hampton the teachers were white. But it was a matter of pride to him that "to the Negro race belongs all the credit of the work accomplished here, and of the judicious use of the funds which the friends of the school, through the efforts of Mr. Washington and Miss Davidson, have contributed."

"Mrs. Washington," he continued, without commenting, of course, on the fact that she was obviously pregnant at the time, "also one of our graduates, is the housekeeper; and the teachers all board with her in a small cottage which they have rented. The table," at which he joined them at meal-time, relishing the food as well as the service, "does not suffer by comparison with that of the teachers' home at Hampton. The farm contains one hundred and forty acres," he noted, pointing to the school's first industry for self-help as well as vocational training, "and the boys were at work clearing a field for sugarcane, which grows well here. They also raise cotton, sweet potatoes, peaches, etc."

Young Booker T. Washington was much too wise to let a visitor like General Marshall leave Tuskegee with the impression that everything was peaches and cream where the school was concerned, however. No inspection, he would have him know, was complete without a look at the quarters in which the boys were housed. So it was toward some of the shacks in which these students were boarding with Negro families of the community that they now headed. Presently the General allowed that the situation was intolerable, just as he and General Armstrong had found this sort of arrangement to be at Hampton a decade ago. He could well understand Booker's deep concern.

Back at his post at Hampton a few weeks later, he prepared for the *Southern Workman* a statement which could not possibly have been timed better. "A building is needed for the accommodation of say one hundred young men, which Mr. Washington says will cost about $8,000 if their labor can be made available in its construction. For this purpose, he proposes to build of brick made on the farm, which has excellent clay. The young men are impatient to be set to work on their building; and, as soon as money enough can be raised to pay the foreman and start the brickyard, it will be put in operation. The wood lot is close to the clay, and fuel can be got for the hauling. Two hundred dollars will secure a foreman long enough to make all the bricks needed for the building. As bricks are always in demand in the town, which has no kiln, it would be a paying, permanent industry."

By the time the May issue of the *Southern Workman* reached the subscribers with the above disclosures, Booker and his associates were getting ready for their second school-closing day. They were preparing to entertain prominent visitors on this occasion, and they were working feverishly to put their best foot forward.

Rain fell in a steady downpour on Wednesday, the thirtieth of May, and fear fell upon the hearts of Booker and Olivia. "Do you think it will rain tomorrow?" they kept asking each other. Neither would dare to answer. The dusty wagon-path to Chehaw had been turned into a quagmire by the time Booker set out to meet the train bringing the main speakers.

Both speakers were ministers, and both came to Tuskegee from Atlanta. Interestingly, one was the Reverend George L. Chaney, formerly of Boston, with whom General Marshall had attended the funeral of Governor Stephens. The other was the Reverend Dr. M. Calloway, until recently connected with Emory College. The first had come to dedicate the new building, which had been occupied since last Thanksgiving, the second to give the school-closing address, but the elements were in a mood of dark merriment as they were driven to their separate places of lodging that afternoon, and Booker's mood was anything but gay.

The sky cleared at night, however, and birds were singing when daylight broke. The ground was even dry enough for an early morning military drill by the young men students. This had been carefully rehearsed, as had the opening exercises and the class recitations, which lasted till eleven o'clock. At this hour everybody assembled in the chapel to hear the Reverend Chaney's "flow of soul," as Olivia called it. This lasted till twelve thirty. By then, the new school building having officially been named Porter Hall, the happy audience adjourned to what Olivia was pleased to speak of as the "feast of reason." It consisted of a picnic dinner for most of those present. For the speakers and a selected few others it was dinner at the home of the Reverend Holcomb, the pastor of the white Methodist Church in Tuskegee.

At two o'clock all reassembled for exciting rhetoricals, similar to those presented at the first school closing a year ago, and the address by Dr. Calloway. What the tired and emotionally spent Booker was thinking by this time can only be imagined, since he made no comment, but Olivia made a note of what passed through her mind as she listened. "As I thought of what his resignation of an honored position among his own race, his acceptance of a work among us, his being here on such an occasion meant for him, as I thought these things in connection with what he is—a man of southern birth, training and sympathies, a feeling of deepest respect for the one who for the sake of a conviction could forego so much that was brightest, and in many respects, pleasantest, and assume so much that is hard and unpleasant, arose within me."

That evening, after "students and friends turned their faces homeward, and the newly christened 'Porter Hall' was . . . wrapped in darkness, and its retired inmates in welcome slumber," she could not help thinking that the school year had been a good one and that the "prospects for the future, though somewhat clouded by the fear of financial embarrassment, are hopeful." A brick dormitory for men, costing at least eight thousand dollars, projected on the assumption that they could make their own bricks and that student labor could do most of the work, was not a thing that even adventurous young teachers could expect to have fall into their waiting hands like ripe fruit from a tree.

Perhaps it would take more than year to achieve this new goal, she mused. But that was the program. There was no turning back now.

7.

Immediately after school closing Booker left for Bullock County to conduct a summer institute for schoolteachers, on the invitation of the superintendent of education. While he was away, Olivia consented to carry on a similar work at the school for some of the teachers of Macon, Montgomery, and Lowndes counties, who were eager to make contact with the spark that seemed to be igniting things at Tuskegee.

After a cool, rainy spring the weather turned miserably hot. Brickmaking got started slowly, following several discouraging failures. Crops of cotton, cane, corn—the three C's of agriculture, as they were called—as well as sweet potatoes and fruit were lovingly cultivated by "Uncle Harry," the old farmer who served the school pending their ability to employ a farm manager as a member of the staff. The advanced students all ventured into the outlying districts in search of teaching jobs in the three-month schools. In the heat and humidity of that summer Fanny's baby was born, and on the first day of September the third school session began with a larger enrollment, and in Booker's opinion, "a much better quality" of student than at any time heretofore.

The enlarged faculty which he was able to employ with the increased state appropriation, plus the Peabody grant, looked promising too. R. S. Pannott, the music teacher from Washington, D. C., was back, as was Mr. J. Maddox, the instructor from Worcester Academy. These, with Booker and Olivia and Fanny, completed the holdovers from the last year. Margaret Snodgrass, the teacher of normal classes and principal of the model school, was replaced by a young woman from Atlanta, Adella Hunt, and her assistant, Lucy Smith, was succeeded by Addie Wallace, another Hampton graduate. Added to the staff was a stalwart and handsome young Hamptonite named Warren Logan; another graduate of the same school, H. Clay Ferguson, whose training and experience fitted him for the position of farm manager, and a third, Miss Rosa Mason, employed as matron and teacher. All told, Booker thought, "the most satisfactory staff we have had."

On the surface, prospects looked fine. But it took Booker less than a month to discover that he had bit off more than he could chew. The new boarding department, which had seemed such a necessary addition, which he had worked and strained to set up in the basement of Porter Hall in time for the fall term, suddenly began to look like a trap to bring about his downfall and the failure of everything he had attempted. True, the place was ready, but tables had to be built by the boys or improvised. There was no money left for tableclothes or enough dishes. Worse still, food cost money, and the school had little or none.

Booker went to town, drawing on his powers of persuasion, and began buying staples on credit.

Back in the teachers' cottage where they lived, Fanny lay ill a long time after the birth of her little girl. Booker began to worry. Word quickly passed around among the people of the community. Professor Washington and his teachers were not getting along well. Storekeepers were talking about cutting off their credit. Negro preachers of the section, who had been sullenly hostile from the start, now began to talk. They had known all the time there wasn't anything to this Booker Washington. They'd give him two years at the most in which to bust his britches and pull out of Tuskegee. All that money he had raised and that property to which his board had acquired title would then go back to the state. An upstart if there ever was one!

Booker didn't try to dispute them. "Had not some of us been at Hampton in its childhood," he lamented, putting the case before his tried and true friend General Armstrong, "and experienced eating with no tablecloth, drinking corn coffee from yellow bowls, seeing wheat bread but once a week, and sleeping in tents, we doubt if our faith would have brought us through thus far." The quotations that came to his mind had to do with "making bricks without straw" and "days that try men's souls."

Scarcely less trying than the situation in the boarding department was the one involving the young men students. After General Marshall's visit, Booker had decided that something would have to be done about them immediately. He could not let them continue to lodge themselves throughout the town, with anyone who could spare a bed. Many of the places they found were unfit. Others were too far away to permit the boys to attend classes at the school and then work on the farm afternoons. Now with the dining hall in operation another difficulty was added. As a solution, Booker had arranged to rent several nearby cottages to house them till the proposed new building could be erected.

The idea didn't seem half bad until it dawned on him that blankets and bedclothing would be needed in these shacks. By then, of course, the boys were all huddled together in their new quarters, their coats hanging on nails, their boots and overalls scattered on the floors, wondering what they would do about the cracks in the walls and the holes in the roofs when winter came. But it was too late to make another change. Booker and the other men teachers came nearly every night to see how their charges were making out, to encourage them and try to keep their minds on the brick dormitory that would eventually be theirs, if they could just hold out.

Another cause for discouragement was the farm. The young crops which had looked so promising at the time of school closing had not done well since. This could be blamed in part on prolonged drought during June and July, but other causes had figured in it, and these, it was hoped, the addition of H. Clay Ferguson to the staff would clear up eventually, though it did not help immediately. Booker had never felt so low since he had first arrived in Alabama, but he was determined not to show a long face to anyone, especially not to his friends back at Hampton.

At least there were good things in sight. When General Marshall returned to Hampton the previous spring, he had not let the matter rest with a few complimentary words. Among the people he had undertaken to interest in the work at Tuskegee was Miss Abby W. May of Boston, and word had now been received that she was sending the school a printing press with all the odds and ends that went with it. It was on the way. While none of the boys knew the first thing about printing, the idea of trying their hands at it gave them a lift.

A new windmill was a boost to everybody. Tendered as a gift through Dr. Atticus G. Haygood, general agent of the John Slater Fund, it could be used to supply all the buildings with water. All that remained was for it to be erected and put to work.

Their pressing needs, of course, far outweighed these gains, and Booker could not deny it. They had finally succeeded in burning one kiln of bricks, and another would soon be ready to burn, but anyone could see they would not be able to make enough bricks by hand really to count. A horse-powered brick machine would have to be acquired somehow, and that would cost two or three hundred dollars.

A carpenter's shop was sorely needed. Given tools, there

was much work which was now costing money that the boys
could do for themselves. Some boys were ready to start
learning the trade.

But the immediate goal was the building. To launch the
campaign for it in earnest, Booker let Olivia return to Boston
for a month of fund raising during November. Meanwhile
he stayed on the job, holding his sick wife's hand when he
could, holding the creditors of the boarding department at
bay when he had to. On one occasion this involved pawning
his watch. Booker was a picture of dejection as he walked
back and forth from the school to the town. On one of these
walks a white woman came to her doorstep and called to
him. Would he please come around to the back door and
chop some wood for her.

She was a Mrs. Varner, owner of an estate between the
town of Tuskegee and the school farm. Up to now she had
not interested herself in the colored folk out there; she was
a survivor of the antebellum planter class, and retained
some of the attitudes of this era toward Negroes. She was
not really concerned as to the identity of the young colored
man with the burdened expression on his face and in his
walk. Nor did she think it out of order to ask a strange Negro to stop and do some work.

Booker looked up, puzzled. After a moment of reflection
he turned and walked around to the back yard. She pointed
to the ax and the woodpile. When he had cut a good pile,
he loaded his arms and began carrying it into the kitchen.
Finally, he put on his coat and continued his walk to the
school.

A day or two later the same woman stepped out of her
carriage in front of Porter Hall and came directly to his of-

fice. She was terribly sorry. She hadn't dreamed, seeing him
walking along the road, that he was the professor. She would
not have spoken as she did, had she known.

But Booker was far too preoccupied by other matters to
care much at the moment. He rose slowly, bowed. "That is
all right, madam," he said vaguely. "I like work, and enjoy
doing favors for my neighbors."

8.

Before any visible change in the school's fortunes could be
marked, Booker began to sense a certain softening of attitude
on the part of businessmen and creditors in the town. But
not till years later did he learn to what extent this was due
to the impression he had made on Mrs. Varner by his hand-
ling of the humiliation she had forced upon him. Mrs. Varner
was convinced that there was something truly extraordinary
about the young victim of her callousness. Perhaps it was a
touch of greatness. In any case, she would never be able to
compensate fully for her behavior. Yet this would not prevent her saying a good word for Booker when the occasion
arose, and where her friends were concerned, the leading
white people of Tuskegee, this could be worth a good deal.

Meanwhile winter came. To get the boys' minds off their
suffering, Booker let a squad of them start digging the basement for the new brick building. Anothing squad began preparing clay to be molded into bricks as soon as the weather
permitted. At the same time he appealed to friends in the
North for money to buy a three hundred dollar horse-power
brick machine which the manufacturer had promised to let
him have for two hundred.

Olivia returned. By the middle of February Booker was
able to announce that funds received from all sources for
Alabama Hall had exceeded five thousand dollars; that the
total needed, as it now appeared, would be ten thousand
dollars. He refrained from mentioning at that time that still
another rift in the cloud, that had hung over Tuskegee since
shortly after school began in September, had now appeared.
General Armstrong, who saw plainly that his protege was in
deep water, had no intention of letting Booker sink. The General
had chosen this time to invite Washington to make a
joint speaking tour with him. They would be accompanied
by the Hampton quartet and several Indian students as exhibits
of Hampton's output.

Hampton, as Booker might have gathered, since Olivia
passed and returned that way in making the trip to Boston,
was certainly in no state of discouragment. Indeed, the opposite
was true. The "imperial Douglass" had just been
there. Nostalgic and sad, but still one of the most impressive-looking
men of his era, the old orator had come before
the student body, in response to the faculty's invitation,
without a prepared speech. He did not expect to talk long.
On the spot, however, glowingly introduced by General
Marshall, he had suddenly been touched by the old fire. The
words poured out.

"I have seen London, I have seen Edinburgh, I have seen
Venice, I have seen the Coliseum, I have seen the British
Museum, but I should not have seen the world if I had not
seen Hampton Institute. I have seen more today of what
touches my feelings, more of prophecy of what is to be, more
of contrast with what has been, than I have ever seen before.

"Only fifty years ago, I was living down here in Maryland
near you, a slave.

"A gentleman once asked me, 'Mr. Douglass, at what college—or institution—did you graduate?'

"I answered, 'From the *peculiar* institution, and my diploma was printed not on sheepskin, but on my own skin.'

"When slavery yet existed, with its rack and thumbscrews and scourge, I could speak, I could denounce, I could appeal; but now that freedom has come to our people, and our country is delivered from that damnable curse, I cannot speak—I don't feel like talking; I feel like feeling—thinking.

"Let us all speak out. No secrets, no dynamite, no revolutions, but a quiet pervading of society with the sentiments of intelligence and civilization. Let these go forth, and they will be the safety of society."

The words were still echoing under Hampton's trees and along the water's edge when in March Booker joined General Armstrong and the traveling group of Hampton students and graduates. Their first meeting was in the vicinity of the Institute. They then moved on to Baltimore and Philadelphia, Brooklyn and New York City, Boston and elsewhere, attracting large audiences at each place. Introduced by General Armstrong at the climax of the program, Booker spoke with deep feeling out of the anxieties and hardships of the months just passed, representing the Normal and Industrial School at Tuskegee as a child of Hampton, an extension of the same work and program, and General Armstrong assured the audiences that this was indeed so and that Booker's efforts had Hampton's unlimited blessing.

No spectacular returns in money were reported as a result of this tour, but a large number of people were reached. General Armstrong expressed the confident hope that "increased interest and aid for Hampton Institute and its 'child,' Tuskegee" would in time be realized. Most important, backed up by the General's prestige, Booker had been introduced to the lecture-going public of big cities in the North in such a way as to make it possible for him to campaign for the school on his own in the future, and before he could get back to Tuskegee, he was making plans in this direction.

He was not able to launch them immediately because the condition of Fanny had grown worse, instead of improving, during his absence. When he reached the school about the first of April, she was seriously ill. News of another kind, that might interfere with any immediate plans to carry out the fund-raising ideas that were turning in his mind, was waiting for him in the mail. Thomas W. Bicknell, president of the National Education Association, had been in one of the audiences Booker had addressed in the East. He was writing to invite Booker to make a speech at the annual meeting of the Association to be held in Madison, Wisconsin, during the coming summer.

Obviously this was a notable opportunity. Not even a bed-ridden wife could consent to his turning it down. Certainly the solicitations for funds could afford to wait while such a distinction as this was bestowed on the principal of the struggling school. Booker accepted promptly.

Meanwhile, Fanny's condition remained about the same until Saturday, May 3. On the evening of that day Booker wrote a card to friends at Hampton saying that he believed a change for the better was about to occur. But he misread the signs. Fanny died the next day.

VI

OLIVIA AND MAGGIE

BOOKER's colleagues at Tuskegee spoke of the "serious bereavement" he had suffered in the death of his twenty-five-year-old wife. They recalled that his "acquaintance and regard for the deceased had begun in their childhood." During the strain of the past year, some of them mentioned, he had repeatedly "expressed the great comfort his family life was to him." Now, seeing the young widower with the baby girl in his arms, their own feelings were touched. Yet, with the possible exception of Olivia, his friends became tongue-tied when they wished to console him. In his thoughts and feelings, all agreed, Booker eluded them. They were obliged to leave him alone. For his part, Booker saw no reason why a personal sorrow should interrupt his work. He began writing the speech he was to deliver at the NEA meeting in Madison.

Meanwhile, a middle-aged mulatto, looking very distinguished in spectacles and fine whiskers, boarded a southbound train at Danville, Virginia, and disclosed to his seatmate that he was on his way to Tuskegee. If there was any question in his mind as to why the white man beside him was so congenial, it was soon answered. The latter was a Hampton teacher (also on his way to Tuskegee) who instantly recognized Richard Theodore Greener from his pictures.

Since his graduation from Harvard with a Bachelor of Arts degree in 1870, Greener had played an active role in an exciting era. Even earlier, however, he had seemed marked for something special. As a boy he supported a widowed mother by working as a porter in Boston. The two had come to that city from Philadelphia when the child was just five. Somehow or other, despite poverty, he had managed to complete grammar school in Cambridge. Two years in the preparatory department at Oberlin had followed. He had then transferred to Phillips Academy in Andover, and from Andover he went to Harvard.

Greener was scarcely out of Harvard when he was made principal of the boy's department of a school for Negroes in Philadelphia, succeeding one Octavius V. Catto, a refined and well-respected citizen, not particularly noted for caution, who was shot in a riot in 1871. At the end of the next year the young principal left Philadelphia to accept a similar position in the Sumner High School of Washington, D.C.

During the few months of his connection with Sumner, Greener had served as associate editor of the Negro newspaper *The New Era*, but in September of the same year he went to work in the office of the United States attorney for the District of Columbia. Two months later lightning struck: he was elected professor of metaphysics and logic in the University of South Carolina at Columbia. Despite the novelty of a Negro teacher in the University of South Carolina, Greener was accepted with good grace and apparently appreciated by his colleagues. He assisted in the departments of Latin and Greek at times and taught courses in international law and the Constitution of the United States. From May 14 to October 31, 1875, he served as librarian of the university and rearranged and prepared a catalogue of the thirty thousand volumes on the shelves. For this he was praised editorially by the *Charleston News and Courier,* and in June of 1877 he read before the American Philological Association, meeting at Johns Hopkins University in Baltimore, a monograph on the rare books in the library of the University of South Carolina. By then, however, the university had been closed by the Wade Hampton legislature.

Meanwhile, Greener had served as member of a commission, whose other members were all ex-presidents of the University, to revise the school system of the state. He had also found time to complete law studies which he had begun in Philadelphia and continued in Washington. He was graduated from the law school of the University of South Carolina "at the head of his class" and admitted to practice in the Supreme Court of that state on December 20, 1876. The following April he was admitted to the Bar of the District of Columbia, and in the same year he became a member of the faculty of the law school of Howard University. Two years later he became its dean. But the deanship was of short duration. He resigned the following year to accept government service in the office of William Lawrence, comptroller of the United States treasury.

While on the faculty at Howard his national reputation was enhanced by two rather spectacular debates with Frederick Douglass on the exodus movement as a way out for the recently emancipated Negroes of the South. One of these was before the Social Science Congress at Saratoga, New York, September 13, 1879, and was reported in newspapers throughout the country. While Greener was no match for the heroic Douglass either in forensics or in personal magnetism, his very appearance on the same platform with the older leader was enough to give him enviable status. In 1882 he opened a law office in Washington and began to take an increasing interest in Republican politics. His acceptance of Booker's invitation to deliver the annual school-closing address at Tuskegee in May of 1884 was a tribute to the good name and prospects of the young school. The visitor from Hampton was properly impressed.

After thirty-six hours the two travelers reached the campus. Soon thereafter, scrubbed and fed and feeling fit again, they were given the usual tour of the grounds and buildings. They were awakened by a gong the next morning, and they were all eyes a little later when the same gong brought the young men students running to their places in line for morning inspection. Marching to drums, the students went to Porter Hall and took their places in the chapel for roll call and devotions. Their singing brought a lump to the throat of the old Hampton teacher.

Breakfast over, Booker took them from one recitation room to another, pausing in each just long enough to catch a few words and perhaps observe the blackboard work. Next they headed for the carpenter shop, the printing office, the brick kiln, the barn, the farm, and the kitchen gardens. Before they were through looking, it was evening, and the students, quietly convened by Booker, delighted their visitors by singing Negro spirituals.

Early the next day the country folk began arriving in carts, wagons, and on muleback. A fine breeze was blowing, and clouds of pink dust rose from the winding roads. As many of the carts were drawn by oxen as by horses, but the smiles of the proud visitors were all the same. Again there was the usual round of classroom visits and industrial demonstrations, and at noon lunch was served in picnic style under four large mulberry trees. A program of essays and orations and music preceded Professor Greener's address in the afternoon.

When the crowds dispersed and the visitors caught the train, Booker returned to the speech he was preparing as the lazy Southern summer settled upon the farm and around the buildings. Hammers could still be heard in Alabama Hall, and when these were silent, Booker could hear the voices of a male quartet rehearsing spirituals.

The young singers were under the direction of a teacher who had himself belonged to such a quartet when he was a student at Hampton. That group, like the one he was now training, had taken a cue from the original Jubilee Singers from Fisk University in Nashville, and used the singing tour to raise money in the North. The interest which the Fisk Jubilee Singers had awakened in this native American music was, of course, a tremendous asset. And even though the Hampton quartet, which ran smack into the panic of 1874, had scarcely realized a net financial gain from their tour, the whole country knew how handsomely the Fisk group had profited, and friends of Hampton as well as of Tuskegee were optimistic about the chances of this group. Their aim was to help raise the balance of some four thousand dollars needed to complete Alabama Hall. They planned to spend the season mainly among the summer resorts of Massachusetts.

Indeed, so warm was their send-off in July that little attention was paid to Booker's departure about the same time. Nevertheless Booker was not unaware of his opportunity as

he began the long train ride from the southern part of Alabama to Wisconsin. He knew what the National Education
Association, which he was to address, represented. He knew
that leading educators from all parts of the nation would be
present. He knew also that important and influential school-
men from Alabama and the other Southern states would be
in the audience. He knew that on the platform he would sit
beside distinguished men with national reputations, and he
might have guessed that the press would be properly represented.

Knowing all this, Booker had written his speech with great
care. But he still felt nervous. He was nervous on the train
going North, and he was miserably nervous on the platform
of the senate chamber of the University of Wisconsin
Wednesday evening, July 16. The twenty-third annual meeting of the National Education Association had begun the
previous evening. Because of an unusually large attendance,
general sessions were divided into three sections meeting
respectively in the assembly chamber, the senate chamber,
and the Congregational Church. On Wednesday morning,
in order to bring the whole crowd together, the meeting had
convened in Capital Park, where the governor of the state
addressed it, and other public officials extended welcomes;
but the evening session had again broken into sections.

While Booker T. Washington was not a name that meant
anything to the delegates as a whole, the question of "The
Educational Outlook in the South" was of burning interest.
Indeed, two of the three sections were slated to deal with it
at the same time. In the assembly chamber William H. Crog-
man, a Negro scholar from Clark University in Atlanta, was
scheduled to give his version at the same time that Booker
was to address the section in the senate chamber. Neverthe-

less Booker's audience was big, and when he began speaking, turning a lead pencil nervously in his left hand, he could see that his hearers were there to weigh every word he uttered.

With a staccato mannerism, which with him was never ineffective, Booker began giving from memory the paper he had written.

Fourteen years ago it is said that Northern teachers in the South for the purpose of teaching colored schools were frightened away by the whites from the town of Tuskegee, Alabama. Four years ago the democratic members of the Alabama Legislature from Tuskegee voluntarily offered and had passed by the General Assembly a bill, appropriating $2,000 annually to pay the salaries of teachers in a colored normal school to be located at Tuskegee. At the end of the first session of the school the legislature almost unanimously passed a second bill appropriating an additional $1,000 annually for the same purpose. About one month ago one of the white citizens of Tuskegee who had at first looked on the school in a cold, distant kind of a way said to me, 'I have just been telling the white people that the negroes are more interested in education than we, and are making more sacrifices to educate themselves.' At the end of our first year's work, some of the whites said, 'We are glad that the Normal School is here because it draws people and makes labor plentiful.' At the close of the second year, several said that the Normal School was beneficial because it increased trade, and at the close of the last session more than one has said that the Normal School is a good institution, it is making the colored people in this State better citizens.

After this statement he changed his tempo to itemize some of the homey ways in which the white community around Tuskegee had helped the young school get started. He would have his hearers know that he maintained rapport with this community by swapping ideas with its leading citizens and following good advice when it was received. He pictured the the white ministers of Tuskegee visiting the school and looking on approvingly as the work progressed. He told of white women baking cakes and giving them to be sold at fairs to raise money for the new school. He gave an illustration of softening racial relationships. "A former slave-holder working on a Negro normal school building under a Negro master-carpenter is a picture that the last few years have made possible," he said casually. But he added quickly.

Any movement for the elevation of the Southern Negro, in order to be successful, must have to a certain extent the co-operation of the Southern whites. They control government and own the property—whatever benefits the black man benefits the white man. The proper education of all the whites will benefit the negro as much as the education of the Negro will benefit the whites. The Governor of Alabama would probably count it no disgrace to ride in the same railroad coach with a colored man, but the ignorant white man who curries the Governor's horse would turn up his nose in disgust. The president of a white college in Tuskegee makes a special effort to furnish our young men work that they may be able to remain in school, while the miserable unlettered 'brother in white' would say 'you can't learn a nigger anything.' Brains, property, and character for the Negro will settle the question of civil rights. The best course to pursue in regard to the civil rights bill in the South is to let it alone; let it alone and it will settle itself. Good school teachers and plenty of money to pay them will be more potent in settling the race question than many civil rights bills and investigating committess.

Again he explained by example. A young colored physician, the first to hang a shingle in the former capital of the Confederacy, was making his way because he was well trained and competent, Booker asserted. "Harmony will come," he predicted, "in proportion as the black man gets something that the white man wants, whether it be of brains or material." That was his creed, and he was prepared to illustrate further. Some of the whites who had automatically turned up their noses at the Tuskegee school at first had been won over by the school's brickyard. These same country folk, he said, came from miles around to buy bricks, which previously had been unavailable in the community. Without calling the name of Lewis Adams, he told how that skilled and enterprising Negro had won respect in Macon County by manufacturing and selling "the best tin ware, the best harness, the best boots and shoes" to be found thereabouts and how, as a consequence, his store was always crowded with white customers.

The educators assembled in the senate chamber leaned forward in their seats. Indeed his power to hold an intelligent audience of this size spellbound was something of a revelation to the twenty-eight year old Booker himself. He had used no highflown language or crowd-pleasing tricks. He was talking in an everyday manner, but the extreme attentiveness of the large crowd was remarkable in every way. A bit more slowly and with a sort of rhythmic punctuation, Booker returned to his main point and repeated for emphasis:

. . . Any work looking towards the permanent improvement of the Negro South, must have for one of its aims the fitting of him to live friendly and peaceably with his white neighbors both socially and politically. In spite of all talk of exodus, the Negro's home is permanently in the south, for coming to the bread-and-meat side of the question, the white man needs the Negro, and the Negro needs the white man. His home being permanently in the South it is our duty to help him prepare himself to live there

an independent, educated citiezn. . . . The teachings of the Negro
in various ways for the last twenty years have been rather too
much to array him against his white brother than to put the two
races in cooperation with each other. . . .

My faith is that reforms in the South are to come from within.
. . . Just here the great mission of INDUSTRIAL EDUCATION,
coupled with mental comes in. It 'kills two birds with one stone,'
viz.: secures the cooperation of the whites, and does the best
possible thing for the black man. An old colored man in a cotton-
field in the middle of July, lifted his eyes towards heaven, and
said, 'De cotton is so grassy, de work is so hard, and de sun am
so hot, I believe dis darkey am called to preach.' This old man,
no doubt, stated the true reason why not a few enter school. Educate the black man, mentally and industrially, and there will be
no doubt of his prosperity; for a race who had lived at all, and
paid for the last twenty years, twenty-five and thirty percent interest on the dollar advanced for food, with almost no education,
can certainly take care of themselves when educated mentally
and industrially.

This was the kind of thinking on which his work at Tuskegee was based, and in conclusion he related what had
been done toward this end in the three years since he started
the school. It was the story of shops and gardens and learning by doing that he had picked up as a student at Hampton under General Armstrong (who was himself in the audience) and applied in the black belt of Alabama.

That the speech had made a favorable impression on those
delegates of the NEA who elected to attend that section was
immediately obvious, but several days were to pass before
its wider impact could be gauged. A woman teacher from
one of the white colleges in Tuskegee went to her room immediately and wrote a letter to the hometown newspaper
saying how surprised and pleased she and the other dele-

gates from Alabama had been by the address. She mentioned the credit Booker had given to the white people of Tuskegee for their help in getting the school started and his generally commendatory remarks about the South. Thanks to her, he found his standing in the local community definitely enhanced when he returned.

But the Madison speech had even more marked results nationally. Newspapers mentioned it in many localities, and invitations for Booker to speak in behalf of his school and on the wider subject of the problem of the races in the South began arriving in surprising numbers and from unexpected directions.

When Booker set out for the engagement in Madison, four thousand dollars had remained to be raised toward the building of Alabama Hall. Within four months after his return the balance was reduced to less than a thousand. It is not clear what part of this, if any, was raised by the quartet of singers, but by the end of the year that campaign was completed and another, this one to raise money for furnishings, had begun with letters from Olivia asking the young ladies of the Framingham State Normal School to furnish one room and the students of her other alma mater, Hampton, another. To this particular endeavor and to many others like it that followed Booker could give only his blessing and encouragement. After July 17, 1884, largely as a result of the impression he had made at Madison, the lecture platform claimed most of his time and energies.

After the Madison speech Booker T. Washington was no longer heard as just another energetic young teacher out to raise funds for his school. His commentary on the overall Southern situation now seemed of some interest. He began to be looked upon, in educational circles, at least, as a fresh new voice. The Tuskegee story, which he continued to tell, was now set in a context. Its meaning widened in the public mind.

Booker was not himself responsible for all of this, of course. A certain ferment in the South and in the nation could be detected. It broke out into the open in January of 1885, six months after Booker's Madison speech, when George W. Cable published a highly provocative article, "The Freedman's Case in Equity," in the *Century*. And it exploded in bitter controversy three months later when the same magazine carried Henry W. Grady's "In Plain Black and White: A Reply to Mr. Cable."

The positions taken by these diametrically opposed Southerners certainly did nothing to clarify the thinking of well-meaning observers in the North. The respected author of *Old Creole Days, The Grandissimes,* and other antebellum novels and stories placed himself squarely on the side of citizenship rights for the emancipated Negroes. He was sick of the silence that had settled over the country in regard to this matter. "All such questions," he warned, "ignored in the domain of private morals, spring up and expand once more into questions of public equity; neglected as matters of public equity, they blossom into questions of national interest; and, despised in that guise, presently yield the red fruits of revolution." Boiling it down, he was opposed to all forms of segregation. "Our eyes are filled with absurd visions of all Shantytown pouring its hords of unwashed imps into the company and companionship of our sunny-headed darlings. What utter nonsense!" He concluded with an observation, "I have seen the two races sitting in the same public high school and grammar school rooms, reciting in the same classes and taking recess on the same ground at the same time, without one particle of detriment that any one ever pretended to discover, although the fiercest enemies of the system swarmed about it on every side."

The thirty-four year old Grady, brilliant and boyish and fast winning acclaim as an orator as well as a journalist, thought Mr. Cable "sentimental rather than practical." He derided the novelist's right to speak for the South, pointing out that Cable was born in the South of Northern parents and asserting that he was not wholly sympathetic with the Southern environment. Grady, on the other hand, was all for separation of the races in churches, in schools, in political life all the way down the line. His promise was that "there is an instinct, ineradicable and positive, that will keep the races apart."

Newspapers picked up the issues as drawn. From one end of the country to the other there was hot comment and discussion. Nowhere, however, was it more intense than in the Negro press. The pages of these partisan weeklies fairly smoked. One correspondent, directing his comment to the editor of the *Christian Recorder,* seemed about as put out with his fellow Negroes as with the younger whites in the South: "The rising generation among the southern whites are being educated to care much less and have less respect for the Negro than their fathers did, many of whom have in former times sucked at the bosom of Negro women. Many of the Negroes had rather be white than go to heaven."

A high-strung young Negro journalist in New York City took a good look at Grady's article and put it aside contemptuously. Bushy haired and light skinned, full of nervous energy, Timothy Thomas Fortune had already crowded a lot of activity and observation into his twenty-eight years. The son of rebellious Florida slaves, his childhood memories

included runaway attempts with his parents in the Ever-
glade country. By 1866, when young Tom Fortune was no
more than ten, his emancipated father was already sufficiently involved in Florida politics to make a move from the
more reactionary western part of the state to Jacksonville
advisable, and it was here that the precocious youngster
went to work as a printer's devil on the *Daily Union.*

When the paper changed hands, Tom lost his job and
entered school. But it didn't take him long to absorb what
Staunton Institute had to offer in the way of education, and
his next step was the city post office. From office boy he was
promoted to stamping and paper clerk and might have gone
higher had his feelings not been ruffled by the postmaster.
He had resigned in a huff and gone back to setting type
when in 1875 he was notified of his appointment as a mail
route agent by Congressman William J. Purman. Working
conditions were not pleasant for a colored boy here either,
but young Fortune bit his tongue and held on for a year.
By that time his congressman friend was able to get him
some sort of special appointment as inspector of customs in
Delaware. His next move was to Howard University in Washington, D.C.

Bent on making a name in journalism, Fortune had come
to New York from Washington in 1881 and taken a job as a
compositor on the *New York Witness.* When he began editing the *New York Globe,* a Negro Weekly, a year later, he
felt like a rabbit in a briar patch. Vowing to "combat error
and arraign opposers of the Negro race before the bar of
public opinion," he began aiming potshots. That some of
them reached their mark and won for him a measure of respect is indicated by his selection within a year's time to
write a book on land, labor, and politics in the South for a

series called "American Questions." Fortune completed his assignment four days after Booker T. Washington's Madison speech, and the book was published later that year under the title *Black and White*. The *Southern Workmen* reviewed it at length, if not quite favorably, in December.

Publication of Fortune's first book coincided almost exactly with the breakup of the three-man partnership that had published the *Globe*. One week later the *New York Freeman* appeared on the streets carrying only Fortune's name as editor and publisher. In one of its early issues Fortune brashly projected himself into the Cable-Grady controversy. "No Englishman has yet written a true opinon of the real condition of the Irish people or of the proper course which England should pursue toward that people," he asserted by way of analogy. "Mr. Grady sees only one side of the picture. All his feelings and interests are centered in his class, and it is the nature of the Southern writer, generally, to magnify the virtues of the whites and the vices of the blacks—the domination of the whites and subjugation of the blacks; instead of the peaceful joint domination of all classes of citizens zealous for the common good. To say that one class of co-equal citizens shall dominate at the expense of another; that one shall enjoy certain public benefits and another be denied; that such a thing as forever keeping separate classes, living as neighbors, having common interests and actuated by like natural and artificial desires—is most absurd and ridiculous."

Fortune called the conditions in the South "highly abnormal." He added a warning. "Mr. Grady pleads that the South be left to work out the race problem as they deem it best and wisest. We have no doubt his plea will be granted. We protest against the lines upon which the South proposes

to work out that problem, and venture to say, if conscien-
tiously adhered to, it will eventually produce results which
none of us honestly desire to see."

Trying to say something soothing in the midst of all this,
the *Southern Workman* reprinted a story it had picked up
elsewhere. "At Trinity church, Staunton, last week," it ran,
"Mary Ann Carter, a former slave, and a consistent member
of that church died. At her funeral a large number of the
white congregation were in attendance, and the fine choir of
the church gave the musical service. The pallbearers were
all prominent white citizens, including the mayor of the
city."

Meanwhile Booker was back at Tuskegee celebrating
Christmas with the students, writing letters of thanks to the
friends who had contributed to the successful campaign to
build Alabama Hall, and getting ready for another round of
speaking in the North. One thing bothered him, however.
Though reaction to his Madison speech had been just as warm
in the South as in the North, no invitations to address white
audiences in the Southern region had been received. This
didn't quite make sense to him, in view of the position he
had taken, but certainly there was nothing he could do about
it.

Meanwhile, too, there was a presidential election and a
return of the Democratic party to power. For a few weeks
Negroes were almost beside themselves with fear. Whether
this would mean a prompt return to slavery, as some predicted, or less complete repression, was not clear, but few
doubted that bad days were upon them. Young Fortune
spoke up promptly:

There can be no backward step. We must go forward. It is the
decree of the Omnipotent. The Democratic Party of today is not

what it was twenty-four years ago. The Democratic Party wants votes, wants all it can get. It will appeal to us for votes. It did appeal to us at the last National Convention. We have the ballot. In the last election the entire Presidential question turned upon two thousand votes [in this] state alone. We have enough votes in New York, New Jersey and Connecticut to decide the election either way. These are the pivotal states. The Democratic Party knows this. We know it. I shall be disappointed if the Democratic Party does not seek to conciliate us. Let us watch events and shape our course in accordance with them.

So disturbed were the rank and file, in fact, that even Frederick Douglass was moved to make a quieting statement from his hilltop home overlooking Washington. The old antislavery hero who had once said, "The Republican Party is the ship, all else is the sea," now acknowledged that he was not entirely without hope for the Democratic Party:

Though it is by history and antecedents bitterly opposed to every measure of justice and equality urged in our favor, it is still composed of men—men with heads and hearts like other men. The world moves and the Democratic Party moves with it. The Democratic Party may not be a good party, but it may be a wise party, and wisdom in statesmanship is sometimes safer than a simple goodness.

Presently the hysteria began to subside. After Cleveland's inaugural address there actually arose among Negroes a feeling of optimism, and as usual Fortune expressed it better than any of his fellow editors:

No class of our citizens [other] than the colored people have better cause to know and appreciate the fact that Mr. Cleveland is a new man with new ideas; and we are much gratified to observe a dawning of the fact upon the colored mind that, in many respects, the Democratic party is not the same as it was under Buchanan, the last Democratic President before the war. In fact, the present is one of surprises to us. The surprises start with the patriotic and statesman-like reference to us by Mr. Cleveland in his inaugural address, and is continued by the party organs and leaders in the broadness and cordiality of their utterances and actions towards us.

Fortune went on to observe the significance of the use of colored troops in the inaugural ceremonies and marked this as "a radical change." "The world moves," he repeated. "1860 and the memories of it are becoming traditions." Some of the new cabinet appointments seemed to be equally hopeful signs. A. H. Garland, the new attorney general, was especially well received by Negroes.

The same wave of optimism inspired comments about the "New South." White teachers from the North who had come South to teach the freedmen had for years enjoyed telling each other the story of the Northern visitor who spoke admiringly of the full moon overhead. "Oh, but you should have seen it before the War," his Southern host replied. Thanks to the influence of such enlightened Southerners as Dr. Jabez Lamar Monroe Curry, agent of the Peabody Fund, President Atticus G. Haygood of Emory University, Mayor Carpenter of Charleston, George W. Cable, and other prominent men of Southern background and blood, that story and others like it were about to become obsolete, some thought. In its place they quoted remarks by Curry to the effect that "slavery, secession, exclusive State citizenship, primary allegiance to a State, are all gone." "The Negroes will now see that not simply the Republican party but both parties and all sections are their friends, pledged to their protection and freedom." Another thing that stuck in their minds was Curry's references to "the dense mass of

Southern illiteracy—forty-five out of every hundred voters; eighty percent of the colored population, and nearly fifty of the white." They joined him in believing that salvation would come with the removal of this incubus of ignorance and in pointing out that every Southern state had by then adopted a school system. Curry and the men who thought and spoke like him were as Southern as possible and as closely identified with the Confederacy as anybody. It was this that General Armstrong had in mind in April of 1885, no doubt, when he referred to "the great uplifting wave of progress" in the South.

Certainly it was to take advantages of this wave that Booker and his associates organized a meeting in Montgomery to help raise money to buy furniture for Alabama Hall. The Tuskegee choir went down to furnish music and Solomon Palmer, the state superintendent of education, proud of his rank as major in the army of the Confederacy, spoke along with the Jewish Rabbi of the city and leading Negro ministers. Of course, Booker's appeal on behalf of his school furnished the climax, and the sixty-five dollars in cash which was contributed by the audience seemed to everyone most creditable under the circumstances.

The occasion also provided an opportunity for Booker to invite Major Palmer to participate in the forthcoming commencement exercises at Tuskegee by presenting the diplomas to the first graduating class. The school was about to complete its fourth year of operation. Ten fine young people, all devoted to the Tuskegee idea, all Christian, were now ready to "carry the light to some dark corner," as Booker put it. What could be more fitting, in view of his policy of cooperation with the white South, than for a well-known Confederate war veteran to pass out diplomas to the first class.

Naturally a Negro of some prominence should be on the platform at the same time. The name of Joseph Charles Price came to Booker's mind. Scarcely thirty years old, striking in appearance but almost blue-black in contrast to Booker's tan, Price's was easily the fastest rising star in Negro America in 1885. Born on Pear Tree Road, just beyond the limits of Elizabeth City, North Carolina, young Price had spent a dreamy boyhood on the banks of the Pasquotank creek, "Where the bull frog jumps from bank to bank," as he liked to remember. Just before the Civil War ended, his free-born mother carried him to New Bern, which by then was free soil. By 1871, when Price was seventeen, he was a strapping youth with a wonderful voice for singing as well as speaking. That year he found employment as a schoolteacher in nearby Wilson, and it was here that he struck up a friendship with a young white fellow named Josephus Daniels.

Daniels was working as a post office clerk, but he attended some revival services where the evangelist occasionally called on "our colored friends" to sing or say a word and discovered that the soloist "had a lute like voice, as sweet as the tones of any bird," and that this same individual, who happened to be the boy schoolteacher, "was an orator who charmed audiences, white and black." Apparently Price himself was not converted at the time. Perhaps the references to "our colored friends" left him cold. In any case, it was after he had gone to Raleigh to attend Shaw University in 1873 that he saw "the smile of God" and decided upon a career in the ministry. Two years later he entered Lincoln University in Pennsylvania as a freshman on a scholarship provided by William E. Dodge, and during each of the four years that followed he ranked first in his class. He graduated as valedictorian and in two more years completed a three-year theological course. Even before completing these studies, however, he was ordained and sent as a delegate to the General Conference of his church in Montgomery, Alabama.

That was one year before Booker arrived in Tuskegee. By then Price was twenty-five and had completely won over J. W. Hood, the presiding bishop. When called upon to speak, he galvanized the Conference. The minutes of the meeting mentioned his "eloquent remarks that brought tears to many eyes." Two years later Price was elected president of Zion Wesley Institute (Lingstone College) of Salisbury, North Carolina, and since then his eloquence had been employed in raising money for that institution. In that work his path sometimes crossed Booker's and there were instances in which an audience, having the choice of either speaker, selected Price in preference to Booker. Competition notwithstanding, however, Booker decided that Price was the speaker he wanted for the commencement address to his first graduating class at Tuskegee.

2.

Booker heard himself referred to rather grandly at these exercises as Tuskegee's "founder." This pleased some of his friends, but his own interest in small talk was slight.

Presently he and Olivia were off on another summer campaign to raise money. When school opened again in the fall, they were able to enroll nearly two hundred and fifty students, about as many as could be handled. Booker's older brother, John, who had postponed schooling for himself in order to help Booker go to Hampton but who had eventually graduated with Olivia's class, was brought to Tuskegee as

"Business Agent and Drill Master," with general oversight of the dormitory life of the boys.

Down in New Orleans Theophile T. Allain, a Negro member of the Louisiana Legislature, announced his intention to present a bill for the establishment in his own state of a school modeled after Tuskegee. Booker felt complimented, and the new school year seemed off to a fine start when four young Tuskegee teachers, en route to a teacher's institute in Alabama, ran into unpleasantness on the train. Aroused, Booker sat down and gave the railroads of the South a piece of his mind. His letter was published in full by the Montgomery *Advertiser,* a prominent Democratic newspaper.

Without specifically mentioning the incident, Booker suggested that mistreatment of Negroes on trains was bad business. "It is not a subject," he said, "with which to mix social equality or anything bordering on it." He had no personal wish to ride with whites, he stated, but only to ride as comfortably for the same money. He wanted to know why respectable colored people paying full fare should be herded into a filthy, crowded smoking car or half-coach with chain-gang convicts and drunken white men. How did the railroads figure that they alone among businessmen were entitled to sell two classes of goods for the same price? Assortment he did not mind, but it should be on the ground of dress and behavior. In Virginia, he pointed out, colored people were not prohibited from riding in the first-class cars. There the poorly dressed Negroes voluntarily went to the second-class coaches. Even an Alabama road, between Selma and Marion, had an arrangement to which he did not object. "Running in one direction the whites use one of these (first-class coaches) and in the opposite direction the colored use the one previously used by the whites—they are equal in all respects."

In any case, Negroes around Montgomery stayed at home nine times for every ten they might travel under different conditions, he concluded. Whether or not his letter provoked serious thought, as the *Southern Workman* seemed to imagine it had, no change in policies on the part of railroads in the direction indicated by Booker was immediately noted. But the line of his own thinking on the whole theory and practice of segregation in the South, later to be reiterated and offered as a basis for racial harmony in the region, and finally to be so widely approved as a practical compromise and to influence a major decision of the Supreme Court and pave the way for a half century of "separate but equal" legislation, was clearly marked. Without realizing it, Booker had epitomized a point of view and an attitude soon to supersede the statements of both Cable and Grady and the editors and orators who echoed them. But at Tuskegee itself there was nothing much to report that year.

More money for the tuition of students who could not pay was the pressing need as 1885 came to a close. In February of 1886 another Montgomery rally was held. Bigger than the first and boasting even more prominent men among the speakers, it brought in a smaller collection. Booker attributed this to "very dull times in the South," but he thought the warm response to the speeches by the more than twleve hundred people was decidedly encouraging.

Having expressed himself publicly on one social issue, Booker used the next lull in Tuskegee news to comment on another. Southern prisons, he observed, were in serious need of reform. The letting of convicts out to private contractors had resulted in shameful abuses. "During the prisoner's entire confinement there are no forces at work that tend to make him a better man when released, but rather a worse one," Booker charged. Moreover, he had observed inhuman treatment of prisoners. One Alex Crews, for example, unlawfully imprisoned in the first place, was so badly used that he dropped dead on the way home after being released. There was the case of the colored boy whose feet rotted off as a consequence of working all winter in a chain gang without shoes. Booker had seen some of these shoeless convicts out in zero weather in Tallapoosa County, and he was convinced the same conditions were general in the South.

Commencement day came, and the second class was graduated. This time the graduates numbered only five, but the orator of the afternoon was the second most distinguished Negro in America, John Mercer Langston. Emancipated as a child in Virginia, Langston had grown up in Ohio, graduated from Oberlin in 1849, and been admitted to the Ohio bar in 1854. With the exception of Douglass himself no Negro had been more effective in the latter years of the abolitionist campaign. After the War, Langston had first served as general inspector of schools under the Freedman's Bureau. In 1867 he was admitted to practice in the Supreme Court of the United States on the motion of James A. Garfield. Two years later he accepted the deanship of the law school of Howard University. In 1877 he was appointed minister to Haiti by President Hayes, a post in which he had remained nearly eight years and from which he had just returned.

Helen H. Ludlow, a Hampton teacher of many years, assistant to General Armstrong in the editing of the *Southern Workman,* and a warm friend of all the fourteen Hamptonians teaching at Tuskegee that year, was one of the visitors to the closing exercises. She found everything wonderful, including the "long and brilliant speech" of John Mercer Langston. Booker might have thought so too, had he not been preoccupied with something else. He had made up his mind to get married again, and the time was approaching. Olivia Davidson, his arden co-worker, his true friend and partner in every trial and achievement since the second month after his arrival at Tuskegee, had consented.

Perhaps some, including General Armstrong and the group at Hampton, had regarded it as a foregone conclusion that Olivia would eventually become his wife, but Booker gave no indication that he had. He made it plain, however, that he had never ceased to marvel at Olivia's enthusiasm and energy despite an apparent frailness of body. The way she had worked for Tuskegee in its first five years was a miracle of endurance and spiritual devotion. She had been at his side during the year of his engagement to Fanny, throughout the period of their marriage, and now for two years since Fanny's death, as a loyal assistant, but with no visible indication that she expected, or that Booker expected her, ever to assume the other's role also. But now at last there was this burst of tenderness.

Olivia, the near-white girl from Ohio (though born at Tazwell Court House, Virginia), the teen-age teacher who had gone down to Mississippi with her brother in the first decade after the Civil War, who had refused to quit her teaching post even after lynchers murdered him, who had offered to return to Memphis as a volunteer yellow-fever nurse during the epidemic, whom Booker had finally met at Hampton, whose training at the Framingham State Normal School in Massachusetts had been sponsored by Hampton's wealthiest patron, Mrs. Mary Hemenway of Boston—Olivia, whom General Armstrong himself had designated as Booker's assistant in the Tuskegee adventure, was to become his wife. Booker disposed of the closing exercises and the graduation of his second class as calmly as he could and promptly turned his thoughts to the new life he was about to begin with his lovely co-worker.

The ten weeks preceeding their marriage in August were not entirely devoted to mooning, however. More requests to speak came that summer than ever before. Audiences, according to a Boston reporter, were "more than usually appreciative." Another noted that "Professor Booker T. Washington of the Tuskegee Normal School in Alabama is still in the city (Boston). Invitations are pouring in upon him from the Unitarian and Congregational people to speak at their churches on the subject of Southern education. Last Sunday, the 11th inst., he delivered an address at Concord, Mass. Next Sabbath, the 18th, he will speak at Derby, Conn., in the morning and at Birmingham in the evening. The National Unitarian Conference which meets in Saratoga, N.Y., on the 20th of September, has asked him to address it."

They were married quietly in the midst of this round of public work, but neither Booker nor Olivia allowed this to alter their schedules noticeably. His first written statement to the *Workman*, following the marriage, however, was perhaps the sharpest protest he ever made. It was occasioned by mistreatment of a group of his teachers traveling as passengers on the Western Railroad of Alabama. En route to Macon, Georgia, where two of them were to be married, "a crowd of roughs came into the first class car where they were riding and told them in a very rough way to go into the second class car. To avoid trouble they obeyed this order."

Complaining loudly to the general manager of the Georgia Central, they were given assurances of protection on the return journey, but at Opelika, Alabama, where they changed back to the Western Railroad, they were met again by the same roughs. Again obeying the order to move into the second-class car, the young bridegroom was struck by a member of the mob as he passed over the platform between the two cars. He continued into the car and seated his bride, but he returned to the platform sizzling. "If it were not under the present circumstances," he shouted, "I would see you all in hell before I would stand such treatment, and I would be willing to go there with you."

For this the young man was arrested, held for about five minutes, given a quick trial and fined for cursing. Exonerating the young man completely, Booker added, "I am surprised that he controlled himself so well." He concluded that Tuskegee's neighboring town of Opelika, from which some of their students came, "has a certain bad set in it. In point of fact, there was so much fighting and shooting there last year among the whites, that the governor was obliged to keep State troops there for a week."

Then for the first time he spoke of Olivia as Mrs. W. and said that she wishes to be remembered. Also he added, "Our saw-mill is up, and we are cutting lumber." A month later he wrote that "Mrs. W. is now in Boston in the interest of the school for a few weeks." "Would love to write more if I had time," he concluded. "All send love." The chopped sentences as well as the rather free use of the word *love* were equally unusual for Booker.

Not again for nearly a year and a half were Hamptonites favored by a general letter from the founder of the school at Tuskegee. And the most exciting thing he had to say to them then was that "Mrs. W., my little Portia, and my little boy Booker T., join me in love to you." But meanwhile no news was good news. Tuskegee was growing up. The peak enrollment had touched four hundred not counting the Training School, and the number of teachers and officers had increased proportionately.

To the closing exercises in May of 1888 came Hampton's chaplain, the Reverend H. B. Frissell, later to succeed General Armstrong as President. He noted that the school property was now valued at eighty thousand dollars and that twenty-three teachers were employed. Nothing impressed him more, however, "than the growth of these Hampton boys and girls," now teaching "under the responsibilities placed upon them." Sharpening his gaze, he made another observation that no visitor before him had caught. "I noticed at the same time that the Tuskegee school was more than a mere copy of Hampton. It has adapted itself to new surroundings, it has taken up new industries, it has, in some respects, improved upon its parent, as any child ought."

New buildings and industries were now old hat, but the Reverend Frissell did find it worth mentioning that Armstrong Hall, the new three-story boys' dormitory, just about completed, had been planned and erected by a Hampton graduate, with the help of students and just one outside workman. And he couldn't help mentioning the job Booker was doing throughout the state by way of educating his constituency. He had influenced their thinking to the point where they now doted on the kind of education Tuskegee offered.

If Booker's own accounts of such matters now came to the *Workman* more infrequently and in sketchier form, perhaps part of the explanation was that he now had a paper of his own on his hands, *The Southern Letter*. But this was by no means his favorite project during the school year of 1888–

89. His heart was in the construction of a new stable which, when completed, he declared "will be the largest and most complete in the state of Alabama."

Booker had loved animals from childhood. A thing that had always galled him in rural Alabama was that "scarcely one man in ten exercises any care for the comfort of stock. The idea that a horse or cow should be protected from the cold, hurtful rains enters the minds of but few; and it is very rare to find persons who curry and clean their animals; hence the animals are weak and of poor quality."

His own horse was now the best he could possibly afford, and the man who was assigned to care for it held one of the major responsibilities of the institution. It was even whispered that one such individual was an ex-convict, parolled by a local judge to the principal of Tuskegee for this purpose, and that this rugged, but grateful and fanatically devoted man, spent the rest of his life in this service, adding also the role of protector and bodyguard to Booker when the times required it.

It was February, and the new stable was coming along fine when still another happy event occurred. Olivia's second son was born. The rejoicing which this occasioned did not however hide the fact that it had been an ordeal for the mother. Olivia remained helplessly weak for days, and before she could rise from her bed misfortune struck. The little frame house in which she lived with Booker and the children caught fire at four in the morning.

Booker was in the North lecturing as usual. When the alarm sounded, some of the older boys came running. Olivia and the young ones were removed, as was some of the furniture, but the cottage could not be saved.

When Booker reached Tuskegee, his wife was still ill.

Weeks passed, and it began to appear that her trouble went beyond the aftermath of childbirth and the shocking experienced which had followed it. Olivia seemed to be in a decline, as they said. There was more than a hint of tuberculosis. In her case this had been feared for years. Hearing about it, Mrs. Hemenway sent a trained nurse from Boston to care for her. A few weeks of close attention convinced the nurse as well as Booker and others that the mere presence of a trained nurse in the house would not be enough to bring Olivia through. When this was reported to Mrs. Hemenway, she arranged for Olivia to come to Boston and enter the Massachusetts General Hospital. Leaving the babies behind, Booker accompanied her. On May 9 she died, and Booker returned her body to Tuskegee for burial.

In Booker's mind, and in the minds of many others, the death of Olivia blotted out the events of school closing and graduation that year, but by fall he was going about his work as usual. Sorrow had done its work, however. To the brisk personality of the energetic thirty-three-year-old educator was added a note of sadness which somehow enhanced his influence. Bereft of two beautiful young wives in the space of five years, he suddenly found himself engulfed in love of another kind. Everyone at Tuskegee seemed to share his heartbreak. Despite his silence and his aloofness, they let him know where they were concerned, he could do no wrong—ever.

3.

One who noticed most sympathetically his sadness and his silence was a striking young teacher named Margaret Murray. She had met him first at Fisk University in Nashville, Tennessee, when she was about to graduate. He had stopped to visit and participate in the commencement exercises. Olivia had been dead just a month. At dinner in Jubilee Hall, the most famous building in Negro education, he had sat at a table with Maggie, as she was known, and other members of the senior class of that college dedicated to the paramount importance of the liberal arts in precisely the way that Tuskegee was not.

Eleven years younger than Booker, erect and poised, radiating physical as well as mental health and energy, a dedicated feminist, soft brown in color and with a glorious head of raven hair, she caught his eye immediately. What he had in mind was a replacement for Olivia, not as wife but as lady principal of Tuskegee. Before the meal was over, he had definitely made up his mind, but Margaret Murray had previously decided to accept a teaching post in Texas.

She was never able to say just how it happened that the plans to teach in Texas were discarded in favor of Booker's offer, especially in view of the lifted eyebrows of classmates who took for granted her commitment to the liberal arts and regarded a decision in the other direction as a kind of disloyalty to alma mater. But the feeling that Booker needed her had prevailed before she was quite sure what drew her. An overwhelming desire to help him with his load engulfed her.

She continued to feel it at Tuskegee that fall, and he must have been gratified by the way it was reflected in her work. But Booker was not talking much.

VII

ARCH ABOVE THE ROAD

A CHANGE in his mood and the fortunes of his work followed eventually, however, and this time the wave on which both rose can only be regarded as historic. Since his address before the National Educational Association in Madison, Wisconsin, which opened up such extensive opportunities for promoting his school in the North, Booker had yearned for a comparable opportunity to make a direct presentation before a representative Southern white audience on behalf of his school and the program for racial harmony which he favored. The opportunity did not come quickly, and when it did, he was a thousand miles away and solidly booked for speaking engagements in New England. Moreover, the invitation seemed at first less than promising.

It was 1893, and the meeting to which he was invited was being held in Atlanta, Georgia. Unfortunately, the invitation stipulated that his remarks be limited to five minutes. It was only after consulting his itinerary and checking railroad schedules between Boston and Altanta that he discovered the possibility of arriving thirty minutes before his remarks were scheduled and catching another train out of Atlanta just an hour later. His final anxiety was whether he could compress enough content into five minutes to make it worth the time and effort. On a hunch, however, Booker decided to give it a try.

The international meeting of Christian Workers, which he faced minutes after arrival, was of course extremely attentive. It numbered about two thousand, many of them Southern whites, and their response was warmly favorable, but it was not until Booker saw the Atlanta papers of the following day that he began to suspect that he had accomplished his aim of getting a fair hearing from the class of whites in the South that he regarded as dominant.

As encouraging as was the response to this rather exciting interlude, Booker promptly resumed his routine work on the road and at Tuskegee and thought little more about it till the spring of 1895. Then, at about the time that the heroic Frederick Douglass was dying in Washington, D.C., Booker received a telegram from "prominent citizens" in Atlanta, as he has described them, asking him to go with a committee to the nation's capital to appear before a committee of Congress in the interest of securing Government help for a proposed Atlanta Cotton States and International Exposition to be held at Atlanta the coming fall. Of the twenty-five members of this committee all were white except three. Booker was one of the latter, and the other two were Bishops Grant and Gaines.

The mayor of Atlanta was a spokesman for the delegation from Atlanta, along with other officials of the city, when they came before the committee of Congress. Eventually the two black bishops were invited to speak, but the last speaker of all was Booker T. Washington, still young, fresh, deeply sincere, who had never before given any kind of speech in the capital, let alone before members of the Congress. Nor was he able to remember afterward any of the words he used when his turn came; but he was sure that the idea he tried to get across was that if Congress wanted to do something that would help to reduce racial conflict in the South and help to make friends among the people, black and white, there could be no better way to do it than by promoting industrial and intellectual growth for both races. In this sense, he felt, the Atlanta Exposition provided an exceptional opportunity. Not since the Civil War, he pointed out, had the Congress been in a position to be so effective in promoting these aims as was now possible by granting the requested appropriation to the Atlanta Exposition.

Subsequent developments left no doubt as to the effectiveness of Booker's fifteen- or twenty-minute presentation. The committee of Congress made a unamimous and favorable report. Following this, Congress passed the appropriations bill promptly. Soon after this action was reported, the directors of the Exposition decided, remembering their debt to Booker T. Washington, no doubt, that it would be no more than proper to put up a large and attractive building on the Exposition grounds to be devoted to showing the progress of black America since emancipation. Moreover it was stipulated that the building would be designed and built entirely by black hands.

I. Garland Penn, a young Negro journalist from Lynchburg, Virginia, was placed in charge of the building, on Booker's recommendation, and the exhibits prepared for display in it were, of course, mainly from Hampton and Tuskegee institutes. All that remained to be worked out was a perplexing question as to the advisability, in the existing climate of almost unimaginable racial hostility, especially in the still-wounded and defeated South, of puttng a Negro representative on the platform to give one of the opening addresses.

Unreconstructed members of the board of directors argued furiously against such a gesture of conciliation and harmony, while other board members ventured to suggest that such deserved recognition would benefit all Southerners in the eyes of the world.

Several days were spent in an effort to collect and evaluate opinion on the disputed issue, but in the end the decision was favorable, and the selection of Booker for the sensitive role was made unamimously. Needless to say, the responsibility it imposed on the young educator from Tuskegee was an almost terrifying challenge. He knew, as he said later, that this would be the first time in the entire history of the Negro in the United States that a man of his color had been asked to speak from the same platform with Southerners on an occasion that could be regarded as nationally important. Fear mingled with a kind of exhilaration as he pondered the anticipated confrontation with the wealth and culture of the white South, his former enslavers, as well as a fair representation of Northern representatives and a certain element of his fellow blacks. What would, or could, he say to such an audience?

While newspapers, North and South, seemed to echo the mixed feelings that had disturbed the board of directors of the Exposition when the question of Negro representation on the platform arose, Booker paced his study in Tuskegee with fear and trembling. Days passed and the opening date approached. He felt like a man carrying a huge stone on his back, a stone which might never be lifted.

The excitement of anticipation was, of course, soon transmitted to Booker's family and to his teachers at Tuskegee

Institute, and it was some of the latter who persuaded him to let them have an inkling of what he was going to say when he faced that massive audience in Atlanta. So on the sixteenth of September 1895, he yielded to their entreaties and gave a sort of run-through in one of the rooms on the campus. The teachers listened gravely, and a few offered criticisms; but most of them heartily approved the speech, and their responses eased Booker's burden of anxiety somewhat. But the next morning, driving to the station in his carriage with his wife and three children, he was stopped by a white farmer who called out, only half-jokingly, "Washington, you have spoken before the Northern white people, the Negroes in the South, and to us country white people in the South; but in Atlanta tomorrow you will have before you the Northern whites, the Southern whites, and the Negroes all together. I'm afraid, Professor, that you have got yourself into a mighty tight place."

Again Booker's fears mounted. The farmer had put it all on the line, clearly, frankly, brutally, and recalling the incident somewhat later, Booker confessed that he began to feel "a good deal as I suppose a man feels when he is on the way to the gallows."

Nor did anything he saw or heard in Atlanta that evening help. The city was agog with Exposition fever. The afternoon papers carried headlines proclaiming the events to follow the next day. The streets swarmed with out-of-town people, many of them in military uniforms or carrying insignia of civic organizations. Booker slept very little that night, and before the sun came up the next morning he was awake and rehearsing the speech which he was prepared to give without reading from his paper.

The morning was still young when a committee came to

escort him to his place in a procession preparing to march to the Exposition grounds. While the carriages were comfortable, the sun became intensely hot and the procession lasted nearly three hours. In fact, by the time it reached the Exposition grounds, what with his growing anxiety added to the heat of the day, Booker felt ready to collapse. Nevertheless, seeing the throngs outside who could not get in and the packed audience, from ground floor to gallery, he must have felt his courage returning. Nor could he have failed to realize that this audience was in part drawn by his presence on the platform, even though it had sometimes been rumored that some of them were there to hear him make a fool of himself.

Meanwhile, among those people who stood outside was one William H. Baldwin, Jr., General Manager of the Southern Railroad, intrepid friend of Booker T. Washington, supporter of his school, and concerned benefactor of his people. His nervousness as he paced the grounds outside was perhaps greater than that of Booker inside, but it was not that he doubted Booker's capacity to perform as the situation required. He was nervous because he could not be sure of the reception this audience and the nation would give to this remarkable Negro in whom he, Baldwin, had such unlimited confidence and to whose work he had committed so much.

Inside, the preliminaries over, facing the thousands of eyes suddenly focused on him, relieving such tension as remained by turning a lead pencil slowly in his hand, Booker began speaking, earnestly, but rather rapidly:

Mr. President and Gentlemen of the Board of Directors and Citizens.

One-third of the population of the South is of the Negro

race. No enterprise seeking the material, civil, or moral welfare of this section can disregard this element of our population and reach the highest success. I but convey to you, Mr. President and Directors, the sentiment of the masses of my race when I say that in no way have the value and manhood of the American Negro been more fittingly and generously recognized than by the managers of this magnificent Exposition at every stage of its progress. It is a recognition that will do more to cement the friendship of the two races than any occurrence since the dawn of freedom.

Not only this, but the opportunity here afforded will awaken among us a new era of industrial progress. Ignorant and inexperienced, it is not strange that in the first years of our new life we began at the top instead of at the bottom; that a seat in Congress or the state legislature was more sought than real-estate or industrial skill; that the political convention of stump speaking had more attractions than starting a dairy farm or truck garden.

A ship lost at sea for many days suddenly sighted a friendly vessel. From the mast of the unfortunate vessel was seen a signal, "Water, water; we die of thirst!" The answer from the friendly vessel at once came back, "Cast down your bucket where you are." A second time the signal, "Water, water; send us water!" ran up from the distressed vessel, and was answered, "Cast down your bucket where you are." The captain of the distressed vessel, at last heeding the injunction, cast down his bucket, and it came up full of fresh, sparkling water from the mouth of the Amazon River. To those of my race who depend on bettering their condition in a foreign land or who underestimate the importance of cultivating friendly relations with the Southern white man, who is their next-door neighbor, I would say: "Cast down your bucket where you are"—cast it down in making friends in every manly way of the people of all races by whom we are surrounded.

Cast it down in agriculture, mechanics, in commerce, in domestic service, and in the professions. And in this connection it is well to bear in mind that whatever other sins the South may be called to bear, when it comes to business, pure and simple, it is in the South that the Negro is given a man's chance in the commercial world, and in nothing is this Exposition more eloquent than in emphasizing this chance. Our greatest danger is that in the great leap from slavery to freedom we may overlook the fact that the masses of us are to live by the productions of our hands, and fail to keep in mind that we shall prosper in proportion as we learn to dignify and glorify common labour and put brains and skill into the common occupations of life; shall prosper in proportion as we learn to draw the line between the superficial and the substantial, the ornamental gewgaws of life and the useful. No race can prosper till it learns that there is as much dignity in tilling a field as in writing a poem. It is at the bottom of life we must begin, and not at the top. Nor should we permit our grievances to overshadow our opportunities.

To those of the white race who look to the incoming of those of foreign birth and strange tongue and habits for the prosperity of the South, were I permitted I would repeat what I say to my own race, "Cast down your bucket where you are." Cast it down among the eight millions of Negroes whose habits you know, whose fidelity and love you have tested in days when to have proved treacherous meant the ruin of your firesides. Cast down your bucket among these people who have, without strikes and labour wars, tilled your fields, cleared your forests, builded your railroads and cities, and brought forth treasures from the bowels of the earth, and helped make possible this magnificent representation of the progress of the South. Casting down your bucket among my people, helping and encouraging them as you are doing on these grounds, and to education of head, hand, and heart, you will find that they will buy your surplus land, make blossom the waste places in your fields, and run your factories. While doing this, you can be sure in the future, as in the past, that you and your families will be surrounded by the most patient, faithful, law-abiding, and unresentful people that the world has seen. As we have proved our loyalty to you in the past, in nursing your children, watching by the sick-bed of your mothers and fathers, and often following them with tear-dimmed eyes to their graves, so in the future, in our humble way, we shall stand by you with a devotion that no foreigner can approach, ready to lay down our lives, if need be, in defence of yours, interlacing our industrial, commercial, civil, and religious life with yours in a way that shall make the interests of both races one. In all things that are purely social we can be as separate as the fingers, yet one as the hand in all things essential to mutual progress.

There is no defence or security for any of us except in the highest intelligence and development of all. If anywhere there are efforts tending to curtail the fullest growth of the Negro, let these efforts be turned into stimulating, encouraging, and making him the most useful and intelligent citizen. Effort or means so invested will pay a thousand percent interest. These efforts will be twice blessed—"blessing him that gives and him that takes."

There is no escape through law of man or God from the inevitable:—

> The laws of changeless justice bind
> Oppressor with oppressed;
> And close as sin and suffering joined
> We march to fate abreast.

Nearly sixteen millions of hands will aid you in pulling the load upward, or they will pull against you the load downward. We shall constitute one-third and more of the ignorance and crime of the South, or one-third of its intelligence and progress; we shall contribute one-third to the business and industrial prosperity of the South, or we shall prove a veritible body of death, stagnating, depressing, retarding every effort to advance the body politic.

Gentlemen of the Exposition, as we present to you our humble effort at an exhibition of our progress, you must not expect overmuch. Starting thirty years ago with ownership here and there in a few quilts and pumpkins and chickens (gathered from miscellaneous sources), remember the path that has led from these to the inventions and production of agriculture implements, buggies, steam engines, newspapers, books, statuary, carving, paintings, the management of drug-stores and banks, has not been trodden without contact with thorns and thistles. While we take pride in what we exhibit as a result of our independent efforts, we do not for a moment forget that our part in this exhibition would fall far short of your expectations but for the constant help that has come to our educational life, not only from the Southern states, but especially from Northern philanthropists, who have made their gifts a constant stream of blessing and encouragement.

The wisest among my race understand that the agitation of questions of social equality is the extremest folly, and that progress in the enjoyment of all the privileges that will come to us must be the result of severe and constant struggle rather than of artificial forcing. No race that has anything to contribute to the markets of the world is long in any degree ostracized. It is important and right that all privileges of the law be ours, but it is vastly more important that we be prepared for the exercises of these privileges. The opportunity to earn a dollar in a factory just now is worth infinitely more than the opportunity to spend a dollar in an opera-house.

In conclusion, may I repeat that nothing in thirty years has given us more hope and encouragement, and drawn us so near to you of the white race, as this opportunity offered by the Exposition; and here bending, as it were, over the altar that represents the results of the struggles of your race and mine, both starting practically emptyhanded three decades ago, I pledge that in your effort to work out the great and intricate problem which God has laid at the doors of the South, you shall have at all times the patient, sympathetic help of my race; only let this be constantly in mind, that, while from representations in these buildings of the product of field, of forest, of mine, of factory, letters, and art, much good will come, yet far above and beyond material benefits will be that higher good, that, let us pray God, will come, in a blotting out of sectional differences and racial animosities and suspicions, in a determination to administer absolute justice, in a willing obedience among all classes to the mandates of law. This, this, coupled with our material prosperity, will bring into our beloved South a new heaven and a new earth.

To say that the immediate response to Booker's remarks that day was tumultuous is to put it mildly. Even the young intellectuals who would later find some of his statements profoundly disturbing had nothing but praise for Washington as echoes from the Atlanta speech spread across the country and rose to an almost unbelievable crescendo. The delayed impact, after the applause and the handshaking subsided, was so shattering as to cause many of those present to miss, or fail to remember, that this was the same Exposition at which a remarkable new invention was first publicly demonstrated in the United States: the moving picture.

Among the hosts of Americans, black and white, who responded by writing congratulatory letters to newspapers in various cities throughout the nation was an astonishingly bright youth named William Edward Burghardt Du Bois, himself just beginning to draw attention as Harvard University's first Negro Doctor of Philosophy. Du Bois tells in his own autobiography how impressed he had been at the time.

A feeling that Booker had said the magic words that saved the nation from calamity, at a frightening moment, began to develop. Few people in their right minds could have believed that waves of terror against black people throughout the country was the way to insure domestic tranquillity, but all, or nearly all, had felt powerless to arrest the drift, which many recognized with horror. Did this mean that it had been left to the principal of a struggling black vocational school in Alabama to pass a miracle that neither politician nor educators nor church leaders had been able to work?

Certainly it began to seem so. Unfortunately, other effects followed his performance later on. The most chilling of these came the following year when the United States Supreme Court appeared to have been influenced by Booker's words and the public response to them. The Court, which had long wrestled with cases involving the civil rights of black Americans, suddenly made up its mind to implement Booker's program: *separate as the fingers*. Of course, it did less, if anything, about the *one as the hand* part, and this may have been the reason its decision in the historic case known as *Plessy* v. *Ferguson* was not unanimous in 1896.

Ironically, too, the new invention which the Atlanta Exposition featured bore bitter fruit for future generations when almost its first significant major film turned out to be an act of out-and-out hostility against blacks in America. And for decades these two consequences of that Atlanta Exposition in 1895 continued to be the affliction of all Negro Americans in the land of their birth.

Out of this dismal backlash came a debate, a great controversy, which began in 1903 when the maturing scholar Du Bois, who had been so prompt to congratulate the "statesmanship" of Booker's Atlanta address, all things considered at the time, set forth his afterthoughts on the man and his work in an essay included in his own book *The Souls of Black Folk*. For about twenty years thereafter debate raged between those who supported Du Bois's criticism and the followers of Booker T. Washington. It was not till 1954 that it became clear to the Court that had given the nation *Plessy v. Ferguson* in 1896 that *separate* was not and could not be *equal* where education or citizenship were concerned.

A year after the 1954 Court decision came the marches of Martin Luther King, Jr. and his contemporaries just forty miles from the station near Tuskegee at which young Booker began his memorable journey to Atlanta sixty years earlier.

INDEX